Heaven Couldn't Wait

Heaven Couldn't Wait

A Little Boy's Legacy

Deborah H. Taylor

Manufactured in the United States of America

Taylor, Deborah H.
    Heaven Couldn't Wait: A Little Boy's Legacy

    ISBN: 1-58244-104-9

    1. Family. 2. Love.   3. Overcoming Loss

Library of Congress Card Number: 00-107628

Contents

*This book is dedicated to the memory
of our son,
Benjamin Lee Taylor*

This is the story of a little boy whose love and courage in his short lifetime knew no boundaries. This little boy was my son, Benjamin Lee Taylor, better known as "Benjie" to everyone who knew and loved him.

Chapter 1

Benjamin Lee Taylor

I first found out I was pregnant on February 1, 1990. We were living in San Diego, California, at the time. I called my husband, Buster, at work, and he was ecstatic. Then, in tears, I called my parents, who were living in Tustin, California, about eighty-five miles north of us, and told them. I loved the idea of being thirty-five years old and pregnant. To have my husband's children was why I got married in the first place. I knew right then that I wanted a boy.

At the end of the first trimester, we lost my mother-in-law to cancer, and so we traveled by pickup to Oklahoma for the funeral. After the funeral, we went on to Wichita Falls, Texas, to visit with my husband's brother and grandparents. They were all very happy about my pregnancy. I can still remember Buster's grandfather, Floyd, who had been sitting with his chin resting on his hand, sitting up and saying, "Hope it's a boy" when we told him that I was pregnant. His movement reminded me of the Life cereal commercial with Mikey, the way he popped up like a toaster. That was early April 1990.

Later in April, I underwent amniocentesis to discover the condition of the fetus, and the gender of the child as well. I had to wait three weeks for the results of the procedure. The three-week waiting period was almost unbearable. Not knowing how my baby was, and yet beginning to bond from the time of the first kick would make any decision to terminate unbearable as well.

I got a phone call the day after Mother's Day from the lab. The baby was healthy. "A healthy what," I asked. "Oh, you want to know the sex?" said the voice at the other end. I was on pins and needles during the silence. "It's a boy! Congratulations!!" I thanked him, hung up the phone, and screamed "Hooray!!" Some of my neighbors came running, believing something was wrong. (We lived in an upstairs apartment of a two-story building.) Then I called Buster at work, and we cried together. He had wanted a boy for so long but had said throughout this pregnancy that he wanted a girl because he had already lost two sons. If it was a girl this time, then he wouldn't have allowed himself to get his hopes up TOO high.

After that phone call, I went running around the complex telling all my neighbors that we were going to have a boy in October. Our friends were thrilled for us. We had lived in the area for almost two years, and they knew of our desire to have children. When we called and told Floyd and Linnie that the baby was a boy, they both cried joyfully.

I could tell you many stories about the playful "fights" Buster and my mom had about the sex of the child. My mom had a knack for being able to tell people what their child would be. She kept telling Buster it was a boy, and he kept saying it was a girl, while secretly wanting a boy.

After talking with Buster, I called my folks and told them that their fourth grandchild, due October 5, 1990, would, indeed, be a boy. In the weeks that followed, I went through the apartment moving glass and other breakable objects to a higher level and putting cleaning and laundry supplies up out of reach. I wanted my home to be as safe for my child as I could possibly make it. Why wait until the child is born to do these things?

I went to the local library and exhausted their sources of information on baby and prenatal care and development. I took reams and reams of notes, filling several notebooks until I thought that I would run out of paper. When that source was exhausted, I bought books on child care. Librarians and bookstore personnel got to know me on a first-name basis, as I became a regular customer.

I had to give up one source of enjoyment while I was pregnant. I gladly gave up bowling if it would mean a healthy and happy baby. Buster didn't want anything to hurt this baby's chance at life. I did, however, continue to go every week and root my husband's team to victory. He was an avid bowler during that time, carrying a bowling average of 165–175. Until the pregnancy, I had carried a 130–145 average.

It was an uneventful pregnancy. Only one-half hour of nausea during my seventh month (July) which occurred at 3 a.m. on a Wednesday morning. I got up, threw up, woke Buster up, and the two of us went back to bed.

Then, on the twenty-sixth of September 1990, I started getting backaches that only increased in pressure as the day progressed. Two days later, after getting Buster off to work, I called my sister-in-law in Oklahoma, who has four kids, to ask her why I was getting backaches. She told me that it sounded like I was in labor and to get Buster home. I told her the back pain was so painful that I couldn't sit or lie down. Nothing helped but heat. She suggested that I get into the shower and let my back soak.

First, I called Buster, but someone else answered the phone. Buster was a field mechanic for heavy equipment, and he was in the locker room changing out of his shoes into his work boots. I told him I went into labor five minutes after he left for work, how much pain I was in, and that he should get home. He said okay. "I'll be home as soon as I can get there." Lucky for me, the company he worked for at the time was only fifteen minutes away. He changed back into his shoes, told his boss what was happening, and left. I was in the shower with the water running on my back when he got home. Fortunately, I had packed my hospital bag a couple of weeks earlier, so I was ready. The only problem was getting me out of that nice warm shower to get dressed and into the car to go to the hospital. While I was getting dressed, Buster took a shower, because neither one of us knew when we would have that chance again.

Due to an automobile accident in which we had been rear-ended four years earlier, my back pain was more severe because of the injuries I had sustained. Thanks to a drunk driver, Buster and I had become two more statistics in the California records on drunk drivers.

Well, I got to the hospital. It was a short ride in mileage, but the trip felt like one hundred miles to my back. I was in total back labor, and my back felt pain with every single bump and rut in the road.

For anyone who has been in labor, you understand what I'm saying. It felt like someone was stabbing me right in the small of my back. We had taken Lamaze classes in preparation for this baby, but Lamaze breathing cannot prepare anyone for back labor.

When I finally got settled into a labor room, I went into the shower as quickly as I could and continued running hot water on my back. I was in the shower for at least forty-five minutes when I reluctantly got out so that monitoring of the baby could begin. They had to run tests that seemed to take forever. I had hoped for a natural childbirth but now I wasn't sure if natural childbirth would be possible. (In Lamaze we were told not to be surprised if labor plans didn't go the way we planned them.) After the tests, it seemed to me that I was now their prisoner and had to do whatever they wanted of me. Nothing my poor husband/coach was trying to do worked. It hurt my husband to see me in this much pain, and he was helpless to end it. I finally gave into an epidural ten hours after I entered the hospital. I had to endure the epidural alone. Buster was asked to leave the room because the anesthesiologist had once seen a father pass out during this procedure, and didn't want to go through that experience again. The nurses were of no use to me. I had hoped to lean on Buster during the epidural, but that was not to be. After the epidural was performed, the pain left. I felt great and became a lot easier to deal with for the duration of the labor.

Eight hours into my labor, my parents arrived from Orange County, which is eighty-five miles north of San Diego. I had called them before leaving for the hospital. They were allowed in the labor room with us, as well as anyone else I wanted to join us.

Around midnight, I signed a release form for surgery. Monitoring showed that the baby was beginning to show signs of stress. I had experienced very little progress with my labor. They had done everything they could to speed up the process, but my body wasn't complying. They declared an emergency situation. I had been the "one of every four" in our Lamaze class who would end up having a Cesarean (C-section) delivery. I got sick only twice during my twenty hours of labor. (Twenty hours went by from the time I called Buster at work until the time of birth.)

Benajmin Lee Taylor made his appearance at 2:44 a.m. on Saturday, September 29, 1990. His father was at my side, dressed in his greens, and proud as a peacock. He was so happy he cried at the birth of our son. Benjamin weighed six pounds, thirteen ounces, and he measured twenty and one-quarter inches in length.

Buster took our son to the nursery and was with him for his first bath. After two hours in recovery, where my parents were allowed to wait since it was a slow night for deliveries, I was eventually moved into a semi-private room at Kaiser Permanente Hospital in San Diego. The care I received there was great. It was my first time in a hospital. The nurses, considering this fact, were very caring and compassionate. They made me feel less afraid and more in control than I thought I could feel. After all, one of them reminded me, I had not only just given birth, but had also had major abdominal surgery. One nurse said that if I felt like crying because of the pain, then I should go ahead and cry. The other nurse told me that I was doing even better than she had done in her previous childbirth experiences. That made me feel better. They truly understood how I felt. In the meantime, Buster and my parents had left to get some sleep and to allow me to do the same, but I was too wired to sleep. Besides, who ever heard of sleeping in a hospital?

Buster had told me that he would be back after noon to see me and the baby, but, when that time came and went, I called him, only to get our answering machine with my own voice on it. Unfortunately, the answering machine was not in the same room as Buster. In fact, there was no phone in our bedroom at the time. So, I called a neighbor and asked him to pound on our door to wake my husband and tell him to call me. Our neighbor, who would become a first time father exactly three weeks later, did as I requested.

Buster called me, and I told him I felt lonely and forgotten. He arrived at the hospital within an hour, and we talked about our plans for our son and how our future with Benjie would be so happy. While I sat holding our son in the chair next to my bed, Buster finished filling out the birth announcements. He would mail them on his way home that night. During the day, I answered all the congratulatory phone calls from friends and family. Buster had even taken the time to write me a special thank you for giving him the son he desperately wanted. He was so grateful to finally have a son in his life. Benjie would become his daddy's little buddy.

After another three days in the hospital, Benjie and I were discharged. The date was Tuesday, October 2, 1990. After visiting with me and the baby in the hospital that day, my parents went home. My back couldn't take another night of the hospital bed. I had begged both the doctor and Buster to let me go home the day before, but Buster wanted to clean the apartment for me and get things organized for his new family. Between trying to catch up on his sleep and cleaning the apartment, he had gone back to work so that he could be available for me for a few days when I came home. Although I could understand what he was trying to do, I was in tears because my back was hurting so much from the bed. Due to the incision in my stomach, I could only sleep on my back, and I was not a back-sleeper. I was grateful to be finally released to continue my recovery at home.

Chapter 2

First Year of Life

Home life with a new baby seemed like a dream come true for us. We both were so happy with our son, just as any new parents should be. We couldn't get enough of him, and we both felt that way, even with the 2 a.m. feedings. I remember the first night. Since Buster wanted the baby to sleep in our bed with us, rather than in the crib in the next room, he could and would attend to him without disturbing me. The first night I awoke to find Buster coming back to bed with a freshly diapered and just-fed sleeping baby in his arms. He knew how exhausted I was and how much sleep I needed. Besides, as he put it, I'd have my chance when he went back to work, and I would be the one getting up during the night to feed and diaper our son. As a new parent, I was glad to have an experienced father in Buster to lend a hand where it was so greatly needed. Besides, his feeling was that since he had been a contributing factor in Benjie's existence, why shouldn't he help in his care as well. Benjie was as much his son as he was mine.

Our family doctor gave us some good advice that I have passed on to other new parents: "Let the child be your guide." That's the best advice any parent can get. As our family doctor would later explain, any physician or medical personnel may be an expert in their field, but the parent will be the expert on that child. No one will know your child better than you will.

After a few weeks of getting used to being a new mom, we finally got Benjie's feeding/sleeping schedule together. Every night, like clock work, he would wake up to eat at exactly 2:50 a.m. I would change him, feed him his bottle, and return to bed, and he would be asleep before his head hit the bed. Slumber wasn't far behind for me either, as I was still mending and needed all the sleep I could get. When the baby slept, I slept as much as I could. Sometimes I would find myself taking advantage of the fact that the baby was sleeping and do something other than sleep, which I would often regret later.

I wasn't allowed to drive for three weeks, and so I had to rely on Buster. I had cabin fever by the end of the first week. I felt that my recovery was progressing quickly until that day when I found myself in the hospital's emergency room.

The doctor had given me a list of things to look for during my recovery at home, such as signs of infection. I listened, but I didn't expect anything to happen. I was healthy and had a healthy baby boy to boot. What could go wrong?

Ten days after Benjie was born, I began "leaking" from my incision. I went to the emergency room, where I was treated, given an antibiotic, and sent home.

When I was finally allowed to drive my own car again, a stick-shift foreign make, I felt like I had been freed from a cage. I could get out, see the world, and show off my newborn son. My first stop was the grocery store. We were out of everything.

At least it seemed that way to me. In the previous weeks, I had to wait until Buster got home, and then we would go out on our errands.

Buster was like a kid in a candy store. Every night, he would walk in and see his newborn son, and say, "Hi, Benjie! Daddy's home." We took videos on the twenty-ninth of every month (or as close to that day as we could) as well as during major events or occasions.

When Benjie was six weeks old, we traveled to Orange County for a special weekend. That journey served a two-fold purpose. My father had suffered a minor stroke in the previous week, and I wanted to check on him as I was not able to visit him in the hospital. The other reason was that my matron of honor was throwing a baby shower for us at my parent's house.

I had been unable to get to Orange County during my father's hospital stay due to a fire close to the freeway. The freeway in that area was closed to through traffic. Because of the freeway closing and the fact that I had a new baby to care for, both my parents felt that I should stay at home. My mother kept us posted on my father's condition. Thankfully, he was released from the hospital the day before the prearranged baby shower.

We received so many wonderful gifts at the shower. A lot of people who had been at our wedding were there. Many of the guests were the mothers of kids I had grown up with and who still lived in the neighborhood.

Luckily, we had a pickup truck with an eight-foot bed. It was packed full of gifts from the shower, as well as a few things we had brought with us for the weekend. We had a new playpen, a walker, and a baby swing to take home, still in their cartons.

At our local swap meet, we had already picked up a very nice stroller bed, a safety gate, and a few other necessities before the baby was born. Something told us to purchase the stroller the week before Benjie was born. As it turned out, the decision proved to be a good one, as I found myself in the hospital the following weekend.

By the time we got home Sunday night, we were tired. Instead of cooking something for dinner, the three of us went out to grab a bite at one of our favorite local restaurants in San Diego.

Each day, Buster went to work, and I stayed at home and took care of our son, going out on errands only when I needed to do so. If I could wait until Buster got home, I usually did. When Buster and I got home from one of our errands one evening, there was a message on our answering machine. The message was to call his boss the next morning before leaving for work. I thought the message was odd, but Buster said it was possible that they wanted to change his assignment. As a field mechanic for heavy equipment, he didn't always return to the project from the previous day. He called in the next morning (Tuesday, November 6, 1990) to find out that he didn't have a job anymore. Here we were with a six-week-old child, and no financial means of support. My emotions and hormones were already out of their normal rhythm due to the recent birth and recovery. I was particularly devastated. Buster wasn't too happy either.

We would learn later that his employer already knew that Buster wouldn't have a job the next day, before he even left the premises. They chose not to tell Buster or allow anyone else to tell him either. Instead, they told him by phone, instead of telling him in person.

I called my folks and told them the news. I didn't know what else to do. My bubble had been burst, and I felt like I was spiraling straight down with no end in sight. Meanwhile, we had decided that Buster would take a day off to enjoy his son before hitting the road to look for a job. That's the kind of guy to whom I'm married. He doesn't just sit around feeling sorry for himself. He's a hard working loyal employee who had just been kicked in the stomach. I have often felt that employers should be as loyal to their employees as they request of their employees. I have found that there is no such employer— unless you're self-employed.

Buster spent the rest of that day checking the want ads and calling to find other jobs that would at least keep food on our table and a roof over our heads. Everything else would have to wait. We had a child to care for, and Benjie was our number one priority. While Buster called and made appointments for job interviews, I did what I could to keep myself busy. We were willing to relocate, but this period was going to be difficult no matter what job opportunities came along.

During Buster's unexpected lack of work during the holiday season, we went to one of the local shopping centers where we came upon Santa Claus. Benjie, in his matching red and white outfit, had his picture taken with St. Nick.

For Christmas 1990, Benjie got a high chair, a walker, his first train, and a personalized quilt. That night, Buster and I both awoke to find that neither one of us had gotten up with Benjie at 2:50 a.m., as we had been doing regularly for weeks. We both immediately checked him to make sure he was okay. We came to the conclusion that he had slept through the entire night for the first time. We considered this his Christmas present to us! He would be three months old three days later.

We ended 1990 without a steady paycheck. Buster worked through a temporary service for the balance of 1990. However, 1991 seemed to get off to a better start. Without our knowledge, Buster's former supervisor had been fighting to get him rehired. Early in the new year, Buster was rehired, and we once again had job security and medical insurance. More important, we had room to breathe.

Benjie was baptized on the seventeenth of February 1991, during the Presidents' Holiday weekend, by the minister who had married us. We drove up from San Diego for the baptism, because we felt that the man who had started our family by uniting Buster and me should be the one to baptize the newest member of that family. I baked and decorated an open-book-shaped cake for the occasion. The inscription on the cake read: "God Bless Benjamin Lee — Baptized in Love 2/17/91."

Benjie continued to thrive and grow each day. By the time he was six months old he was crawling. He learned to crawl backward before he crawled forward. I came home from shopping one day to find Buster had put him in his walker. Benjie's legs were so strong that Buster felt it was time to start exercising them, and Benjie was doing just that. He could make that walker move.

When he was about six months old, we entered Benjie in the San Diego Area Baby Show of 1991. He scored 97% (third place) in the beauty division and 100% in the health division for his age group. We were later presented with certificates commemorating those achievements.

I had a Golden Retriever, "Oly," before I got married, and on Easter 1991, he was already twelve years old. We recorded on videotape that dog allowing Benjie to literally crawl all over him. Oly did not move a muscle to stop Benjie from crawling over him. He trusted me not to let anyone hurt him, and, in turn, I trusted him not to hurt my son. Benjie received his first rocking horse for his first Easter, among other gifts.

Benjie walked with help during his seventh month. He made being a new mom so easy. He was so easy to care for, as he very rarely complained about anything. You never knew when he was cutting teeth. He never got cranky. It seemed like one day he didn't have a tooth, and the next day he did.

In May 1991, when Benjie was almost eight months old, Buster decided to take his vacation. We went by pickup to Texas. Buster's grandparents were now in a nursing home, and we wanted them to meet their only great-grandson.

It took two days to get there. Although Benjie was a very tired little boy, he turned out to be quite a good little traveler. As long as he was with his mama and daddy, Benjie would go anywhere. His only complaint was the same as ours—his seat got hard.

By this time in his life, Benjie was beginning to eat solid foods. This particular week he ate peas, so feeding and traveling were easy. Being left handed, I could easily feed him while we were on the road. That way, we would keep moving, and he could eat and then sleep. That kid slept very well in his car seat, or anywhere for that matter. From a very early age, he had to have skin contact before he would fall asleep. He would rub my arm, under the sleeve, up and down. As he fell asleep, the rubbing would slow down until it stopped, at which time he was sound asleep.

After two days on the road, we got to Buster's brother's house. He had two horses—a chestnut-colored stallion, appropriately named "Red," and a young bay filly named "April"— she had been foaled one day in April. Red whinnied in Benjie's face, and he just laughed. He wasn't the least bit frightened, and, as it turned out, became good friends in a very short time with Red. We soon learned that Red was very gentle with people but often fought with other horses. April kept her distance. She was a pet to my brother-in-law. Neither horse was broken in to ride. I took a picture of the two horses, and people thought, as I did, that it was a perfect picture-postcard photograph.

The next day we went to the nursing home where Buster's grandparents resided. It was the Tuesday before Mother's Day. Buster's grandmother, Linnie, was so happy to finally hold Benjie's small hand that she cried tears of joy. At age eighty-eight, she had glaucoma and couldn't see but was thrilled nonetheless. Buster's grandfather, Floyd, on the other hand, could see, feel, and talk to his great-grandson, and he did. Not only did he talk to Benjie, but he made sure that everyone who could, came into their room to see and meet, as he put it, "his boy." Next to Benjie's beaming father, you never saw a prouder man than Floyd Taylor. Whenever anyone came into the room, I remember Floyd saying, "That's my boy, my great-grandson. He came all the way from California to see me." He was as proud as a peacock. I took a picture of Floyd and Benjie together. A week after that visit, we lost Linnie. She died on the Tuesday after Mother's Day in 1991. She had held out just long enough to meet her great-grandson. (Six days after his ninety-seventh birthday, on July 1, 1991, Floyd took a nap and never woke up again.)

From Texas we went to Clinton, Oklahoma, to visit with Buster's sister and her family. Her oldest child's name was also Benjamin. He was twelve years old and couldn't keep his hands off his little cousin. They were all thrilled to finally meet him and play with him. We spent a few days with the family and then traveled home.

By the time Benjie was eight months old, he was standing. It took about another month for Benjie to master sitting up, crawling forward, and walking on his own. This all took place by the tender age of ten months. By the time he was ten and one-half months old, he was off and running and, from that time on, he never looked back.

He was a healthy, happy, little boy who, except for a cold and his allergy to corn, with which he had a love-hate relationship, was never sick. He loved corn, but it hated him.

Benjie's first birthday was celebrated with two parties, one in Orange County at my parents' house and another at our home in San Diego with our friends. We took Benjie to Disneyland the day before the birthday parties. He had his picture taken with Mickey and Minnie Mouse, Brer Fox, and Roger Rabbit, and he even sat on Donald Duck's lap. The next day, Saturday, September 28, 1991, we had a party for him at my parents' home where we played games and ate cake and ice cream. He looked so cute with cake all over his face. He was a mess! We had a huge turnout for his first party, with many of my friends and their kids, as well as family members. I opened Benjie's gifts for him. Then we had another party for him back in San Diego when we got home. I decorated the cake for that party with three primary-colored balloons.

As he had at Christmas, Benjie made out like a bandit with gifts of toys and clothes galore. The love our family and friends showed our little boy told us how much he meant to a lot of people. His love and devotion would emerge in ways we never thought possible in a child so young.

Chapter 3

Second Year of Life

His personality really started to blossom at this time. He wrinkled his nose whenever he smiled. It became his trademark.

In October of 1991, I threw a surprise fortieth birthday party for my husband. That day, we had decided to have a family portrait done to give to my parents as a Christmas gift. That plan fit right into my surprise party for Buster. I had two neighbors get everything organized and decorated while we were gone. Needless to say, he was surprised. Benjie was the most thrilled of all. Today, that portrait hangs on the kitchen wall of my parents' home.

For Halloween, Benjie was a dinosaur. He tired out after a few doors.

At fourteen months old, he played hide and seek. He loved to look for Daddy. Buster would discover some interesting hiding places, usually right under Benjie's nose.

In December, he "helped" his daddy put Christmas lights

up around the front living-room window of our San Diego apartment. Whenever Buster put the hammer down, Benjie would pick it up for his daddy.

For his second Christmas, Benjie received a junior activity gym from my parents. He mastered the slide before the morning was over. During the day, he bounced on my brother's knee.

He didn't think much of the clothes he got that year, but then, at fourteen months old, why would he? His attitude would change as he grew older.

He had a very long attention span for a child of that age. That characteristic became evident to us on Christmas Day. He received a new book and sat in a corner looking at it for almost an hour. He looked at the book while sucking on his pacifier.

As for his Christmas take that year, he again made out like a bandit. His activity gym became his favorite place to play or just to sit.

One day I walked into his room to find him in his toybox. His toys were scattered all over the floor. He was seventeen months old. He loved to play chase and would initiate a game at any time.

At eighteen months old, Benjie had his first pony ride at the grand opening of a local indoor swap met. He cried so much at the end of the ride that we let him have another ride.

We had an egg hunt for Benjie at my parents' house for Easter 1992. In the backyard, he ran around with my Golden Retriever "Oly." Benjie thought Oly was great, and Oly had a great fondness for Benjie. Benjie ran around that day holding onto Oly's tail. Oly didn't seem to mind at all. There was a special bond between the two of them that only they understood.

At nineteen months old, Benjie seemed to blossom. He had several accomplishments. He got his first skinned knee; he could partially dress/undress himself; and he declared his independence from me. He could catch a ball thrown to him and throw it back with some accuracy. He enjoyed "helping" me clean our apartment. He could feed himself, and even was able to correctly name parts of his body when asked.

In May we traveled to Texas to visit with Buster's brother and his family. We were there for about a week. They lived in a trailer on their property. One night, the four adults went to play bingo while Buster's niece, Brandi, stayed home with her daughter, Ashly, and Benjie.

After playing with Ashly for a while, Benjie got very quiet and walked over to the cooler at the door. (Brandi had placed a cooler across the open front door so the kids could get some fresh air.) Brandi noticed Benjie at the door, and asked if he was all right. Suddenly, he started crying, and he couldn't stop. He wanted his mama and daddy and was afraid we weren't coming back. When we did get home and found our distraught little boy, he told us his fears and wouldn't let go of me. It took two hours to calm him down.

In June, Buster brought home an orphaned kitten whose mother had been killed on the college campus where he worked. Benjie had a special talent for handling a young animal. He was very gentle with it, and the kitten, although somewhat wild, responded in kind.

On the sixteenth of June, we took Benjie to the annual Del Mar Fair in Del Mar, California, about twenty miles north of San Diego. There was an organization in Del Mar called "Ident-A-Kid Services of America." They provided identification cards for children. We were always very protective of our child, especially in public, which is a sad commentary on today's society.

For the Fourth of July, we had a Kentucky Fried Chicken meal and picnicked on the tailgate of our pickup at the airport in San Diego, otherwise known as Lindbergh Field. Benjie really enjoyed these times and had an uncanny knack for identifying the different airplanes coming in for landing. His favorite was Southwest Airlines. The two reasons we could think of for his preference were that they landed the most frequently and that they had one particular airplane painted to resemble Shamu, the killer whale of Sea World.

As it got too cold, and the sun went down, we turned the truck around, and sat inside the cab and continued to watch the incoming planes. However, we put off retreating to the pickup as long as possible by wearing sweat pants to keep the cold away. Even on the hottest of summer nights, the airport was often chilly since it was located directly across the street from San Diego's Embarcadero waterfront.

Benjie, at the tender age of twenty-one months, played the Nintendo game "Tetris" and soon had a record of twelve lines. Also at twenty-one months, he learned to say "no," and it became the primary word in his growing vocabulary.

On July 22, 1992, Benjie suffered his first loss. Oly had to be put down. That little guy cried for three days over that dog. Even though Oly didn't live with us, Benjie's love for Oly was deep.

At twenty-two months old, he began to talk on the telephone to his daddy and grandparents. At this time, his vocabulary began to grow on a daily basis. His enunciation was considerably clear for someone so young. He also began to learn manners, beginning with learning to say "thank you."

During his twenty-third month, we took him to the San Diego Zoo. He loved animals so much that he couldn't get enough of them. However, his body gave up on him, and he fell asleep on the way home. He also learned the word "I." He started to show a hand preference. He would be right handed like his daddy.

For his second birthday, we drove to my parents' house. We left right after Buster got home from work the night before Benjie's birthday. I had everything packed and ready to go, so that all we had to do was put our belongings into the truck and get rolling. That Friday, we took him to Disneyland in Anaheim, California, for the second time. He walked all over the park and was still tired the next day at his party.

The theme for his birthday party was "Teenage Mutant Ninja Turtles." He had loved them ever since the age of one. He even had a turtle birthday cake. The "turtle" gifts he received included two "turtle" shirts and a video. He also got his stuffed Teenage Mutant Ninja Turtle "Leonardo," who would later become known as "Buddy." Buddy was as big as Benjie, and they became inseparable from that moment on. He got a 1-2-3 bike and his first Tonka truck. My parents gave him a wooden-sided red wagon.

By cake time, he was getting tired. He'd eat cake and rub his eyes. Eventually, he had as much cake on his face as in his stomach.

We all slept well that night and went home the next day, as we had to get ready for the work week ahead.

Chapter 4

Third Year of Life

For Christmas of 1992, we gave him a black rocking horse. He named it "Midnight." My parents gave him a Little Tykes railroad train. Practically every gift he got was Teenage-Mutant-Ninja-Turtle-related. He got a sleeping bag and comforter, videos, a turtle tent, and shoes.

In February 1993, we took a short trip to Las Vegas for a weekend getaway to celebrate Valentine's Day. We stayed at Circus Circus and just enjoyed being a family.

At my nephew's first birthday party in March, we announced that Benjie would be a big brother in November. We were hoping for a girl this time. Even Benjie hoped for a little sister.

As my pregnancy progressed, so did my little guy. He insisted on being my personal secretary and answered the phone whenever it rang. I couldn't get up too quickly at times, so he took it upon himself to do it for me. He proved to be quite efficient, as he would screen my calls for me, asking the identity of the caller if the voice did not sound familiar to him. If they didn't sound familiar and wouldn't give their name, he would hang up on them. He hung up on my sister, as she was not a frequent caller.

Easter fell on the eleventh of April that year. Again, Benjie had a fun egg hunt in the backyard of my parents' house. He found all the eggs and didn't want it to end.

In July, Benjie suffered another loss. He was a Nascar race fan, as we were at the time. We had our favorite drivers. Benjie didn't learn his numbers the conventional way. He learned them the "Nascar" way. He could tell you the numbers one through twelve and the name of the corresponding driver for each of those cars. His favorite, however, was number twenty-eight, Davey Allison. Davey Allison was also an avid helicopter pilot. He and another man were flying his helicopter when it experienced mechanical failure and crashed on its side. Davey died the next day without ever regaining consciousness. Benjie cried uncontrollably, and he couldn't understand how Davey could leave him.

After that, whenever he saw a Texaco sign, he'd yell out "Davey Allison!" Texaco had been Davey's sponsor and his car wore the emblem of the company.

As we had on the previous year for the Fourth of July, we had a Kentucky Fried Chicken meal and picnicked on the tailgate of the pickup. However, this year we had our picnic on the college campus where Buster served as custodian to the school's power plant. Besides, the view from the top of the hill was spectacular, especially on a clear day. As it got cold and the sun went down, we turned the truck around and got inside the cab to wait for the fireworks show that we would be able to see from that location.

Benjie got so excited watching and waiting for the show to begin that he tired himself out and fell asleep in my lap before it started. He missed the whole show. He woke up just long enough to get back into his car seat for the ride home.

We took Benjie to Knotts Berry Farm in Buena Park, California, on the seventeenth of September to celebrate his third birthday. When we first entered the park, Benjie and I talked to the miner while petting his burro. We went on a few rides as a family. Because I was pregnant, I couldn't go on many of the rides, so Buster went on them with Benjie. The rides in the dark scared him, and he would hold onto me for dear life. For that reason alone, he hated the mine-train ride. He and Buster went on the parachute jump. Benjie loved it so much they went up again. Then, we went on the carousel.

While Benjie and I watched, Buster went on the ride "Montezuma's Revenge." Benjie had a lot of fun looking for his daddy.

Next came the big rigs, and, in Camp Snoopy, Benjie went on the "Octopus." He went on the Octopus alone. Next, he and his daddy went on the camp bus and the roller coaster. He loved the hot-air balloon ride. The three of us went up in the SkyTower above the parachute ride for a bird's-eye view of the park and the surrounding area. After that, we had a pretty tired little boy.

The next day, we had a family birthday party for him. We had a game to see who could guess the number of candies in the jar. Everyone participated, child and adult alike—that is, everyone except Benjie and his cousin John. They were practicing their somersaults in the living room.

His birthday cake read: "Happy Birthday Benjie," and it had a rainbow on it. His cousin Billy helped him open the

tightly wrapped gifts. He received a bowling set, a Mary
Poppins video, a Viewfinder and slides, turtle videos, a Cootie
game, flash cards, a turtle communicator, monster cars,
Matchbox cars, a toy binocular set, a blue Crayola lamp for his
bedroom, a tire-shaped case for Matchbox cars, and a red tri-
cycle with a bell on it.

After opening the gifts, we cut the cake and enjoyed it. A
short time later, a college friend of mine, Alicia Ludolph, and
her son, John, arrived to enjoy the cake with us.

Benjie had good table manners for a three-year-old. He
would wipe his mouth often, and he even wiped, or tried to
wipe, John's mouth on occasion.

On his actual birthday, Buster and I took him to a Chuck E.
Cheese pizza parlor to play games of skeeball and have pizza.
We all had fun that night and Benjie didn't want to leave.

Chapter 5

Last Year of Life

On the ninth of October 1993, Buster and I went to my twenty-year high school reunion. It was great to see all my former classmates. Some had changed so much, while others I recognized immediately. Poor Buster couldn't dance to the song I requested because his knees were bothering him so much. Knee injuries were an occupational hazard of his job. He felt bad that he couldn't dance, because it was our song.

Benjie had a great time spending the evening with his favorite cousin, Billy, my brother's son, at my parents' house. When we got home that night, Benjie was so wired. He didn't want Billy to go home.

Everyone had been asking me when the baby was due, and I told them five more weeks. However, Tiffany Nicole Taylor had other ideas. Instead of being born on November 20 when she was due, she made her appearance seventeen days after the reunion, on October 26. Her initials, TNT, suited her well.

Benjie was so good the night before. He had gone to bed around 9 p.m., and, while I was lying in bed watching TV, my water broke around 10 p.m., and I started labor. I wasn't packed for the hospital as I thought I had plenty of time. I had thought that Benjie and I would pack during the next week. We had to wake up Benjie at 11 p.m. after I hastily packed my bag for the hospital. Crying a little and with his turtle Buddy in his arms, Benjie got into the truck with us for the short ride to the hospital.

He only cried twice after he heard me get upset. As soon as I talked to him, he settled down once again. He slept when I slept, and he "coached" me when his father coached me. After Tiffany was born, and the doctor was leaving the room, I told Benjie to wave bye-bye. He waved, but he also said, "Bye-bye, thank you for my Tiffany." In response, the doctor asked how old Benjie was, and he couldn't believe that he had only turned three the month before. He thought Benjie was at least five due to his clear speech and size. At Tiffany's birth, he was three days shy of being thirty-seven months older than his sister.

The boys went home that night, and Benjie slept in my bed so that he could be as close as possible to me. Tiffany and I would come home the next day.

For Halloween, he wanted to be a Ninja turtle, so I took him to the Target store near our home in San Diego. We got him a turtle costume, complete with a red head band, which was Raphael's color. He knew all the colors and names of the Ninja turtles, and I eventually learned them all too.

That night, Buster took him around our complex, while I stayed home with Tiffany who was now five days old. To my surprise, they were gone for quite a long time. Benjie, I was later told, was enjoying himself so much that he conned Buster into taking him to other buildings within our complex.

The next day, on November 1, Buster lost his job again. Tiffany was only six days old. Benjie had been six weeks old when Buster lost his job the first time.

A week later, we found ourselves in Las Vegas, Nevada, again. This time, we stayed in my girlfriend's apartment to save money. Tiffany was two weeks old. We were in Las Vegas for a job interview at the Caterpillar dealership in town. By the time we left at the end of the week, we had a pretty good feeling that we would be relocating to Las Vegas.

By the time she was three weeks old, Tiffany was sleeping through the night. Benjie had been three months old when he accomplished this.

On the fifteenth of December 1993, when Tiffany was seven weeks old, we moved to Las Vegas, and Buster started his new job a few days later. On the day that Tiffany turned three months old, Buster was once again unemployed through no fault of his own. We would later learn that he had been set up for this fall. At this time, he decided to make a career change and look into other lines of work.

Our Las Vegas apartment was great and very comfortable. It felt quite cozy, and I thought we would be there for years. For just a few dollars more in rent, we had a second bathroom, a third bedroom, air conditioning, a dishwasher, covered parking facilities, and a walk-in bedroom closet with a light. We also had a patio/balcony overlooking the street. We didn't have that in our San Diego apartment, and we had lived there for five years.

Benjie was a perfect big brother. I couldn't keep him away from Tiffany. He wanted to feed, hold, and play with her. Several times I found him in her playpen so that he could be close to her. Benjie loved Tiffany so much that it hurt him when we wouldn't let him get close to her.

We traveled to California for Christmas so that Tiffany could have her first Christmas with her grandparents and the rest of the family. My birthday in January 1994 was special since my family took me to a nearby hotel on the Vegas strip for a prime rib dinner. It would prove to be the best birthday of my life.

When the opportunity arose, we had identification cards made for the kids. In a local shopping center, Benjie and Tiffany both had their pictures taken, and we put them on I.D. cards. Tiffany's I.D. card was made for the first time, and Benjie's was updated.

Buster started professional truck-driving school in April, so we couldn't get to California for Easter. We had the egg hunt inside our apartment, where I hid a number of eggs for Benjie to find. I had to hide them a second time since he was having too much fun to quit. Later, I took pictures of the kids with the stuffed Easter bunnies they received from their grandparents in California. Later, after all the excitement had ended, Benjie fell asleep on the sofa with his sister. I took pictures of that too. They were always so cute together.

In early April, before he started truck-driving school, Buster and I took Benjie to Disneyland, and we left Tiffany with my parents in California. After all the sacrifices he had made on his sister's behalf, we felt he had earned a day at the Magic Kingdom. We all had a blast that day, but Benjie couldn't wait to get home to Tiffany.

Later in April, Buster and I went to Bally's Hotel on the Vegas strip to see the Oak Ridge Boys in concert. I had been wanting to see them perform ever since they first came to my attention seventeen years earlier. The kids stayed at home with my girlfriend and her daughter. We had close to front row seats, and the show was fantastic. I hated to see the evening end, but all good things do.

Living in Las Vegas, we had to get used to the dry heat of summer, as well as the thunderstorms with lightning. One night in July, I was sitting out on our patio/balcony in my sand chair. Buster was at driving school that evening. He still had a few more weeks of classes. Tiffany was in her playpen inside the cool apartment. Benjie joined me but stayed just inside the door, where he felt safe. Benjie decided to come out on the patio with me, while I watched the lightning show in the sky. It was still light out, and the rain had not started yet but was threatening. Benjie made himself comfortable on my lap, with a blanket around us. Every time the lightning bolts would hit, he would hide his eyes in my neck. By the time he looked up again, the next one was striking. He never looked up when there was not lightning. When it started to rain, we moved inside. We brought in almost everything on the patio. The wind picked up, and the weather report called for flash floods as well.

For the Fourth of July, Buster made a last minute decision to take us out to the Silverdome in Las Vegas to watch the fireworks show. After parking the car in a decent spot, we sat and waited for the show to begin. Again, Benjie fell asleep before the show started, and so he missed the fireworks again.

A few days later, on Friday, July 8, we took the kids to the Ringling Brothers and Barnum and Bailey Circus. The show was held at the Thomas & Mack Center on the campus of the University of Nevada, Las Vegas. The highlight of the show was two baby elephants born less than a year before. At half-time, Benjie was ready to go home, but, with a little persuasion, he agreed to stick it out. When the show was over, he was the most upset. He realized that he had loved every minute of it.

On Wednesday, July 20, Benjie was invited to his first non-family birthday party. It was held for the little girl who lived below us in the downstairs apartment. Her name was Krista Pollard, and she was five years old. She also had a sister named Tiffany, who adored our Tiffany. At that party, I really got to know our neighbors, and when the party was over, we felt like we had known each other for years, instead of for only a few months. Their friendship would later shine through like no friendship should ever have to do.

On August 5, 1994, Buster got his commercial driver's license, and I threw him a small surprise party to celebrate. This one he appreciated. However, the surprise was on me, since he came home earlier than I had expected. Not everything was ready when he arrived, but we had fun just the same.

Four days later, the kids and I put Buster on a plane. He would be in training for his new job for six weeks, and so we wouldn't see him for at least that length of time.

Benjie got upset and nervous. He spoke of his thoughts and said that he would never see his father again, but he did, on August 20, 1994.

Chapter 6

Tragedy Strikes

I awoke earlier than usual, at around 6:30 a.m., that Saturday morning, August 20, 1994. I guess it was because I knew that I would be seeing Buster. After all, we hadn't seen each other since the kids and I put him on a plane ten days earlier. The kids were still sleeping. Benjie slept until about 7:45 a.m. Tiffany woke up soon after that.

Buster called at about 7:30 a.m. to say that he would be in Las Vegas in about three hours, at 10:30 a.m. our time (PDT, Pacific Daylight Savings Time). I said okay, the kids and I would be ready anytime after 10 a.m.

By 8 a.m. we were all awake. Benjie wanted cereal, and so he ate the last of it. Since the cereal was gone, I told him I'd fix him pancakes the next morning. His response was "That's a good idea." Next, with Benjie's help, or rather insistence, I fed Tiffany her rice cereal, and then I put her down in her pen with her morning bottle.

While she had her bottle, I got dressed and got Benjie

dressed. At first, he insisted that he wasn't going, but I won that battle. He often argued with me about leaving the house, and I somehow always got past his refusals one way or another. By 10 a.m. we were all ready and raring to see Daddy. But 10:30 a.m. came and went. Benjie took his father's delay in stride. Around noon, when Benjie finally asked about his father, I told him that it was just taking Daddy a little longer to get here than he had expected. Benjie accepted that explanation and went back to watching TV. Then, he got hungry and asked me to fix him a Miracle Whip sandwich, and I did. In fact, I made Benjie his third sandwich before we left the apartment after Buster called at 12:47 p.m.

By 1 p.m. we were on our way to pick up Buster. Benjie kept asking, "Are we there yet?" We had to drive south on I-15 from Las Vegas to the Blue Diamond off-ramp to meet him. He was on his way to Tulare, California, by way of Barstow, and so he stopped at the 76 Truck Stop for lunch and fuel. When we finally got there, we saw him out in front of the truck stop waiting for us. I lowered my window, and he reached in and gave me a kiss. Then he got into the backseat of the car. He had to go to the post office and get a money order for his training driver, and I needed one too. On the way to the post office, he got reacquainted with Tiffany who remembered her daddy very well. Benjie was half asleep by then. Buster gave each of the kids a hug and a kiss.

We arrived at the post office, and Benjie lagged behind the whole way. He had been so excited to see his daddy again, and he just relaxed after seeing him. The hot August sun didn't help his energy level. The highest mercury reading for the day was already around 110° F with promises of hotter temperatures before the day was over. I had to prod Benjie out of the car and encourage him to catch up with us as we walked into the post office. He readily took my hand as we walked inside. We got our money orders and left. We were in and out of the post office in less than five minutes. Then we drove back to the truck stop where Buster directed me to his parked truck.

We all got out of the car. I got my camera out of the diaper bag, and then I joined my family in the cab of the truck. Benjie was already sitting behind the wheel of the rig pretending to drive us somewhere, anywhere.

Buster showed us his home-on-wheels, where he had been living the past ten days. It was impressive. Following a short camera session, during which I took a picture of Benjie behind the wheel of the big rig and then some photos of Buster and the kids alongside the truck cab, we got back into the car and drove to the front of the truck stop and parked in the auto parking zone. We got out, went inside, got a booth, and sat down to order lunch as a family.

Benjie wanted to do everything the way his daddy did. He ordered iced tea, and he had to have Sweet'n Low in it rather than sugar. He didn't know why, except that the pink packet was the one his daddy used, and that was good enough for him. He wouldn't even let me put a straw in it so that he could drink it the way he had in the past. That wasn't the way his daddy drank, so Benjie wouldn't drink that way either. After all, Benjie had been the man of the house for the last ten days, and so he would drink his tea the way the only other man of the house drank his—with Sweet'n Low and without a straw. Surprisingly, Benjie was very neat and didn't spill a drop. He also ordered a grilled cheese sandwich and fries on his own. The waitress asked me what he wanted, and I told her, "He just told you." He sounded clear to me. His father asked him if grilled cheese and fries were what he wanted, and Benjie confirmed his order. Buster and I both ordered our meals, and the waitress left. Buster fed Tiffany her meal. She had been sitting quietly in her carseat/carrier, looking at and listening to her daddy. Benjie sat next to me, and Buster and I were across from each other on the aisle of a window booth.

A few minutes later, our meal arrived, but the waitress didn't bring Benjie's, and he lamented, "Hey, where's mine?" I told him, "Be patient. She only has two hands, Honey." She brought his meal on her return trip, along with the ketchup. I had French dip, and Buster had chicken-fried steak.

While eating our meal, we discussed Buster's experiences during the past ten days on the road, and we filled him in on what had happened at home. We all just enjoyed being a family, together again. While we were talking, Buster's training driver, who had been across the street at the new "Boomtown" Hotel/Casino, approached our table. His name was Mark Purdy. He tapped me on the shoulder like I had known him for years which broke the ice. I said, "Hi Mark. Glad to meet you." He and Buster playfully chided each other, and then Benjie very carefully explained to Mark that he had sat behind the wheel of Mark's truck and "drove" it. Benjie went on further to explain that he didn't use any keys, but he sat in the driver's seat just the same. While he was talking to Mark, he was using his hands to emphasize his explanation. Mark asked Buster if he had given Benjie a ride in the truck, and Buster said no. He said that the truck was too crowded, and there was not enough time since Buster and Mark had to leave pretty soon. So, we finished our meal and talked a little more, and Buster promised to give Benjie a ride next time. Mark talked to Tiffany for a few minutes while Buster paid the tab, and then we all got up and went out to the car for our good-byes. They were not easy. Buster put Tiffany into the front carseat and belted her in. Benjie and his daddy gave each other a hug and a kiss, and Benjie got into the car next to his sister in the front seat. Then, it was my turn. Buster and I hugged, but I couldn't let go. Buster had to practically pry me away from him. I would have hugged him for the rest of the day, but he had to go, and so did I.

I got into the car. Buster and I kissed once more through the open window of the car, and, as he walked back inside the truck stop, he yelled over his shoulder, "I'll call you again in twenty-four hours." I said okay. I started the car, and turned on the air conditioning to keep the kids cool. The seatbelt was too hot for Benjie, so I had to help him put it on. Then I put my seatbelt on and we prepared to leave. Then, I got the idea to sit and watch Buster's truck pull out, and I told Benjie my idea. Of course, he loved it. So I pulled over where I thought we would be out of the way, sat, and waited. We saw Buster walk around the trucks, and then he went back inside the truck stop. Finally, when I thought they would never come out, we saw Buster and Mark walk out of the truck stop at about 3:10 p.m. A few minutes later, we saw the truck pull out of its space, and, while we watched and waited, they drove around the back of the building to the side street past our vantage point. As they pulled across in front of us, Benjie and I waved to his daddy. Buster waved from the passenger side, and Mark waved from behind the wheel. It was 3:20 p.m. by then. We pulled in behind the truck at the light. The truck made a left turn at the green light, and we did too. We raced to get alongside the truck in order to get one last chance to wave good-bye before the truck would veer off to the right and enter the southbound freeway. We would continue straight to get on the northbound side. We didn't reach the truck in time, but the truck sounded its air horn, and I told Benjie that the sound was his daddy's good-bye to him. With tears in my eyes, I said, "I love you, Babe." Benjie reassured me and said, "It's okay, Mama. He'll be home again soon." No one could know how prophetic that statement was.

We needed some things at Target, so the kids and I went to the store on the southwest side of town. Benjie fell asleep with his pacifier in his mouth on the way. I woke him up when we arrived. He had only slept for about twenty minutes. As he got out of the car, he handed me the pacifier saying, "Here Mama, I don't want everyone to see what a big baby I am." That's when I knew my baby boy was growing up, but to me, he would always be my baby boy. As we got his sister out of the car, he told me that his favorite colors were blue and red—they were the colors of his two favorite Teenage Mutant Ninja Turtles.

Benjie wanted to play video games, one of which featured his beloved turtles, so I said okay. "You play these, and I'll do my shopping, but don't leave here without telling me where you are." We had learned the art of compromise, and it was making our lives delightful. He said okay, and I went over two aisles, got what I needed, and was back where I had left him in less than five minutes, only to find that Benjie was gone. I called out to him, and he answered me. He was at the other end of the aisle playing with the sample Sega system. He had discovered that the Nintendo system was not working properly. When I told him that it was time to leave, he put up a little resistance until I explained to him that I had let him do what he had wanted, and now it was his turn to do as I asked. With that, we checked out.

As we were leaving the store, Benjie was walking on the right side of the cart, and he was holding onto it as well. Over his shoulder, he asked me if I was proud of him, and I very proudly told him that I was. It had gotten windy while we were in the store, and so he held the cart close to the car for me while I put his sister into the front seat. When I saw that it was getting too windy for him to control the cart, I told him to go ahead and get into the car. I would finish putting our purchases in the car and then join him and his sister. I told him to keep an eye on her for me, which he gladly did. At the same time, he would be out of harm's way and safely in the car.

After we got home, we all changed into our nightclothes, or at least I did. Benjie was notorious for shedding his clothes the minute he got inside the house and running around in a diaper or pullup, whichever he was wearing at the time. That was a standard practice for him. We were all hot and sweaty, and I thought we should get out of our clothes, turn up the air a little, sit down, and cool off. I had already put Tiffany into her walker so that she could stretch her legs after being in her carseat/carrier for the past several hours.

I bought Benjie a Mighty Morphin Power Rangers coloring book at Target. He wanted to color and asked me to get his crayons, and I did. He sat at the kitchen table in his daddy's chair and proceeded to color. He mentioned to me that he was staying on the paper. I praised him, since nine times out of ten he was very careful to keep things neat and clean. Then, he realized that one of his favorite shows on Nickelodeon was on and raced down the hall to our bedroom to watch it.

Before too long, the phone rang, and I made the mistake of answering it. It was about ten minutes after 6 p.m. Benjie came running down the hall to the kitchen. He saw that I was already on the phone, and I said, "It's Grandma. Do you want to talk to her?" "No," he said, with his arms crossed in front of him, and he stormed off in a huff. My mom and I talked for a few minutes. She had tried to call a couple of times before and got no answer. I reminded her that we were with Buster, and then she remembered and asked if we had had a good time. I said yes and filled her in on the day's activities. We gabbed for a few more minutes, as only mothers and daughters will, and said our good-byes. Then I sneaked down the hall to check on Benjie, and he was lying on our bed watching TV. He never saw me. He was so entranced by the show that he was watching. He was also half asleep, with his nose rubbing back and forth on his Ninja blanket. He would be asleep soon since I had interrupted his earlier nap to get him out of the car at Target. He always rubbed his nose back and forth with his blanket before going to sleep if he wasn't sitting in either my lap or his daddy's lap and rubbing our arms up and down. As sleep would overtake him, the rubbing would slow and eventually cease altogether, and we would know that he was out like a light.

Secure in knowing that he was okay, I went back to the living room to see what, if anything, I could find to watch on the TV. I settled on "Major Dad," which had started at 6:30 p.m. and I also began sorting our the kids' latest portraits. Ever since Benjie's first portrait, we regularly sent copies to all the aunts, uncles, and grandparents.

At 6:54 p.m. the phone rang again, only this time Benjie didn't come running. I called him, but he didn't answer. I assumed that he had fallen asleep again, as he had one earlier in the car. By the time I answered the phone, it had rung three or four times. Surprisingly, it was Buster calling from

Lenwood, California, from the truck stop outside Barstow. We talked for a few minutes, and he asked why Benjie didn't answer. I told him that I thought he must have fallen asleep on our bed as I had seen him there earlier. I said, "Hold on. Let me go check on him." I put the phone down and what happened next is every parent's worst nightmare.

With Buster waiting on the phone, I walked down the hall to our bedroom. As I entered the room, I could see that Benjie was not on the bed. I said, "Hey Benjie, where are you?" I was expecting to hear him say, "In my room, Mama," but I got no answer. I went further into our bedroom where I found what would drastically change our lives for the worst forever.

I found my precious little boy hanging by his neck from the vertical-blind cord in our bedroom. I let out a blood-curdling scream that Buster could hear from the kitchen phone. I don't remember holding Benjie in the hallway. All I can remember is lifting his lifeless fifty-pound body up and away from the cord. His eyes were half open, and his face was already turning purple. Then I screamed, "Oh my God, Benjie, not my little boy. My baby, please, not my Benjie!!!" His eyes were half open and glazed over. I had enough presence of mind to know that I had to attempt CPR as soon as possible.

When I entered the kitchen, I screamed into the phone, "Buster, I've got to call 911. Benjie's hung himself." I heard, "What?" and disconnected with Buster. I called 911 as soon as I could. I had laid Benjie down on the kitchen floor and started mouth-to-mouth resuscitation and CPR. The 911 operator answered. I gave my information—name, what happened, address, and the nearest cross street (with correct spelling). Somewhere along the way, my REACT training had kicked in. The operator tried to tell me how to give CPR. I told her I was already doing it. I knew how to do CPR. I had taken a class with a girlfriend when we lived in San Diego. I felt like the operator was hindering my attempts to save my son. At the same time, I was afraid of hurting him by pressing too hard on his chest and possibly doing further damage to his lifeless body.

I remember being on my elbows with the phone on one shoulder and lying on the floor on my stomach. Tiffany was in her walker running over Benjie's left arm, and I had to keep pushing her off of his arm. I'll never forget giving him that first puff of air and hearing that eerie, hollow sound it made as it came back out of his lungs. It was a haunting sound that will stay with me for the rest of my life.

It seemed like only a few seconds had passed, and the paramedics were pounding on the door. I didn't even hear them the first time. By the time I opened the door, they were yelling at me to open it. Frankly, remembering the damn door was the last thing on my mind.

Earlier, while I was on the phone with the operator, I heard the call-waiting tone, and I knew Buster had to be trying to call back; I later learned it was. I was on the phone with the 911 operator and ignored the beep.

The paramedics came in and rushed past me to the kitchen where Benjie lay. They yanked Tiffany out of the way and moved Benjie into the living room where they had more room to work.

A lot of what happened is still a blur. I remember confusion and commotion. There was a lot of yelling—back and forth. I do remember yelling downstairs to my neighbor to take Tiffany out of harm's way. In getting her out of their way, the paramedics had put Tiffany, still in her walker, near the open

front door. Since we lived upstairs and our door was at the top
of those stairs, I was worried for her safety. Diana Pollard, my
neighbor, didn't hesitate. She came upstairs and took the baby
for me, easing my mind and allowing me to concentrate on my
other child.

Diane's husband, David, also came upstairs in a flash and
was at my side. He even stood up to a paramedic who told him
to leave. David stood his ground, saying that he was there
because he had promised Buster that he would look after us
while my husband was on the road. Because of that promise,
David had every right to be there. I also told the paramedic
that David was there at my request because I needed a friend
to rely on and for moral support. Then, I was called into my
bedroom with the police and had to leave the room. When I
returned, I learned that the police had ordered David to leave
or face arrest for interference with an officer. Diana later told
me that David came downstairs looking and feeling like a
dejected puppy because he had not been allowed to help out in
the way in which he had promised.

A few minutes later the phone rang. It was Buster. He
asked me if Benjie was breathing. After I told him what happened and said that I didn't know, I asked a paramedic. I could
hear the desperation in Buster's voice, and I felt it too. One
paramedic said, "We're breathing for him, ma'am." I couldn't
see Benjie, except for his feet, as he was surrounded by big
men.

Benjie had three favorite TV shows: "Walker, Texas
Ranger," "Cops" and "Rescue 911." He loved the fact that he
could see "Rescue 911" every week night and twice on
Tuesdays. We would watch it together. I was often tickled by
the way he would lecture me on what he learned from each

episode. It also made me very proud. He used to sing the "Cops" theme song when it played. However, his all-time favorite show was "Walker, Texas Ranger." It made him feel closer and prouder of his daddy. Buster is a former USMC Gunnery Sergeant who earned a Sixth Degree Black Belt in Karate while in the Corps. He's also a native Texan and one-quarter Cherokee. Benjie loved the idea that the star of "Walker," to him represented his daddy. He didn't realize at his tender age, that Chuck Norris was a karate champion several times over. All he cared was that Walker used karate to bring in the bad guys and he did it in Texas. He liked the idea that there was something on TV to which he could relate.

Our apartment was filled with paramedics and cops. He would have been ecstatic except that he was legally dead, or clinically dead, at the time, but I didn't want to give up hope. I told Buster to get home as fast as he could. I asked him not to drive home. If he had to, he could ask the California Highway Patrol to fly or drive him. He asked me what hospital Benjie would be going to and I told him UMC, University Medical Center, which is associated with the University of Nevada, Las Vegas. Buster said he would get home as soon as he could, and hung up.

I told one officer (I think his name was Mike Finley) that we didn't have any health insurance, and he told me that in a life-threatening situation such as this, that didn't matter. The hospital would have to help him. That made me feel a little better.

I was called back into the bedroom, and when I came out, they said, "If you're going with your son, you'd better get down to the ambulance." I didn't have any shoes on; I didn't have my purse. I asked if I could get these things, and they said, "No, it's leaving now. Go. Go. Go." The officers told me they would lock up the place for me.

The ride to the hospital took about six minutes. It was freezing in the ambulance. I had trouble getting into it because it rode so high. Everyone outside was staring at us, wondering what was going on with this little boy on the stretcher. I saw the coverage on KVBC News later on. The trip seemed to take forever. I couldn't bear to turn around and look at what was going on behind me. It hurt too much to watch what they were doing to my little boy. To make matters worse, traffic did not stop for the ambulance, even though the siren was going. Instead, the ambulance had to stop to prevent an accident. As we got out of the ambulance at the hospital, it finally hit me, and I started crying. We had passed a funeral home, and I remember saying to myself, "Please God, don't let it come to that." I couldn't believe this was happening to us. It was a bad dream, and it was only going to get worse.

Before we left for the hospital in the ambulance, I had been grilled by three cops. First one cop grilled me, then another, and finally a third. I thought I was going to be arrested. My rights were even read to me. That's what really scared me into thinking they were planning to arrest me. Besides, I felt so guilty. I don't know why, but I did. I couldn't explain it to myself at the time, and I'm not sure that I can now. As a parent, when you see your little one lying there so helpless, and you're helpless to help him, it can really get to you. After all, you're not superhuman.

Once we arrived at the hospital, Benjie was taken to the emergency room. When the hospital personnel figured out that I was his parent, a nurse named Caroline approached me, took me by the hand, and led me to a private waiting room. She sat with me and held my hand until a woman named Mona from the Volunteer Trauma Intervention Program arrived. Mona sat with me, held my hand, and acted as an intermediary between the doctors and me. She said that she would stay with me until Buster could get there. I told her what was going on. I was freezing. I was barefoot. She said that I was in shock. She got me a blanket and some water, and sat with me. I told her I'd like to make some phone calls. She let me use her cellular phone. I told her I would call collect. I wanted to call my brother. Mona offered to dial the phone for me. I told her that if she got my brother's answering machine she should tell the operator that this call involved a life-and-death matter so that the operator would allow me to leave a message. Then, I would make it a person-to-person call, and the operator would have to let me leave a message. Mona dialed and the next thing I knew she was talking to my brother. I heard her say, "Wilson Hart, (pause) I have an emergency phone call from your sister, Deborah Taylor. She's sitting right here waiting to talk to you." I got on the phone with Bill. I said, "Bill, I'm here at UMC with Benjie. We've had a terrible accident. I found him hanging in the vertical-blind cord. I had to give him CPR, and I don't know what to do. I need you to go over and tell Mom and Dad so they don't hear it by phone. I don't want them to hear this by phone." (Benjie was their favorite grandchild. They had been at his birth in San Diego.) My brother said he would take care of talking to my parents. I had called him at about 9:45 p.m. Then, I called my sister, Christie, and told her what happened. She asked me if I wanted her to call the folks, and I told her that Bill was going to tell them in person. I said, "Christie, it doesn't look good. They say we're going to lose him." I said that I'd keep her informed. Nobody got much sleep that night. Next, I called my neighbors to check on Tiffany. Diane Pollard told me that the cops wouldn't allow her or David to go inside our apartment. I asked the officer who was taking a statement from me to contact a fellow officer at my apartment. I asked them to allow my neighbor to go in the apartment to get the necessary items for Tiffany's care. Officer Finley, who was with me, talked to Officer English, who was with Diana at my apartment. Diana was on a cordless telephone and could hear my officer talking to hers over the radio. After Diana got the items she needed, she took Tiffany over to her mother's house to be with Diana's three kids. Diana's kids knew that something had happened to Benjie, but they did not know the seriousness of the situation. Then, the Pollards brought me my shoes and my purse.

As I was finishing the police statement, I was called into the room where Benjie was so that I could see him before he was transferred to the Pediatric Intensive Care Unit (PICU) across the hospital's parking lot. I told the cop that I felt like this was all my fault. He told me, "Don't, this was just a horrible accident." Then I went to see Benjie. When I came back, I hunted Officer Finley down so that I could sign his statement. No one had ever done that before, and he thanked me. Then, I went back to the ER waiting room.

Before I went back to the ER, the doctor came in and told me that Benjie was in critical condition with severe brain damage. The next twenty-four to forty-eight hours would be critical. However, they didn't expect him to survive even until the next morning, August 21, which was less than twelve hours away. They also told me that he was in a deep coma.

When the doctors said that they wanted me over at the PICU, the seven of us walked over—the two detectives, Officer Finley, Diana and David Pollard, Mona, and I—in the 100° heat at around 10:30 p.m. Feeling the need to hold a friendly, masculine hand, I asked Diana if I could hold David's hand. It was obvious that I didn't have Buster's hand to hold. She said, "Sure, Deb, go ahead." She knew how much I needed that comfort, and David didn't feel that he was doing much good, but he was, just by being there.

After that short walk, we entered the PICU, and they said that I could go in and see him. Every time we wanted to go in, we had to either call ahead or get the attention of one of the nurses in the unit through the window in the door, because the door was locked. The door limited visitor access, but it was wide open when we got there. Before I was allowed to go in, the detectives wanted to talk to me again, and they led me into the waiting room on the floor. I was once again questioned about what happened. They didn't even know about my second child until David Pollard mentioned that his relatives were taking care of her at the moment. I said, "What good does this do my son?" They said that they needed to know different things for their report. (I had heard one cop say earlier, "I wish my wife kept our place this neat." Everything had been cleaned the day before, with Benjie's help.) Everything was repeated over and over again. As they would say in court, "Asked and answered." All I kept saying was, "Please let me see my baby. I just want to see my baby boy."

He was the only person actually classified as an ICU patient. All the others in the unit were Intermediate Care (IMC). I started talking to him. His vitals were taken every hour, whereas the other patients' were taken every two hours. They would probably go home the next day.

Chapter 7

The Vigil

Benjie was hooked up to so many wires and tubes. They had put a diaper on him. I remember seeing the X rays of his pelvis in the Emergency Room. My neighbor, Diana, told me that the cops read the letter that I was writing to my sister-in-law. They read it from beginning to end. They looked at all the pictures on the walls. While I was talking to Benjie, I heard someone say, "Dad's here." With that, I looked up and saw Buster in tears, walking down the hall toward us. Mona was with him. I walked out to meet him. It was about 11:30 p.m. I said, "I'm sorry." He said, "It's not your fault." I felt at the time that it was. We were holding each other and crying together. Benjie was the third son that Buster was going to lose, and I was the mother of that son. He went into Benjie's room, looked at him, and said, "Hi, Daddy's here." We kept hoping against hope that God would grant us a miracle and let our little boy live. Buster rubbed his eyes, took off his glasses, dried his eyes, and said to the doctor, "Okay, I don't care how much it hurts, I want to know the bottom line. What's going on here?" The doctor said, "Let's talk out here." They went out of the room and down to the end of the hall, leaving me with our son. I continued talking to Benjie.

The doctors told Buster what was going on, and then he came back to me. I said, "What's going on?" He took me by the hand, led me to a conference room, sat me down, and placed my hands in his. I knew by the look on his face that whatever he said wasn't going to be good. He said, "The bottom line is, we're going to lose him." I immediately fell into his arms and put my face into his lap, saying, "I know.' My miracle child was going to be taken away from me, and I had nothing with which to fight for him. There was nothing I could do to help him.

After we had a chance to console each other, and visit with Benjie together, Buster and I left his room. Mona was standing by. She told me that as soon as Buster appeared at the back door of the hospital, a clerk had approached him to ask if we wanted to donate Benjie's vital organs after his death. She told me that she chased the guy away, as Buster was too upset to even think of a response. Buster would tell me later that he would have decked the guy if it hadn't been for Mona. However, Mona did threaten to do just that. I could only think about what was going through Buster's heart at that time. The guy was talking so nonchalantly about donating organs, and Buster hadn't even seen Benjie yet. Some people can be such vultures. Only a heartless person could ask such a question of the grieving.

At about midnight, I called Bill again. He immediately told me that he and Allison had been talking, and he'd come to the hospital the next day. I said, "Bill, Benjie is dying, and there's nothing I can do about it. He may not make it until morning.

He may be dead by the time you get here, even if you fly." He said he was driving. I told him to please be careful, as I didn't need to worry about him too. Then he told me he would be bringing Billy along because Billy and Benjie were so close. Benjie was Bill's only nephew, and Benjie had been like a little brother to Billy.

Then I called Christie again, and told her that Benjie was dying and that he probably would not survive the night. She said that the doctors could be wrong. After I made the phone calls, Buster held me while I cried.

Meanwhile, Bill went back to our parents' house and told them. Bill would later tell me that when he appeared at my parents' kitchen window the first time, they couldn't figure out what he was doing at their house at that hour of the night, especially on a Saturday. Then, he told Mom and Dad. He said, "Little Ben's had an accident" and told them what happened. He went back to their house at midnight and told them that it didn't look good. I wanted to tell them myself, but I didn't want to tell them by phone. They were both elderly—in their late seventies—and he was their favorite grandchild. How do you tell a grandparent that they have to say good-bye to a grandchild? It should be the other way around.

All of the doctors said that Benjie would not live until morning. They said that he would be brain dead by the next morning, but he wasn't. Sunday morning, August 21, he was still alive. His breathing was not regular, however, even with the respirator. I said to the nurse, "Why isn't his breathing in a regular rhythm?" Her answer was, "Because he's fighting the respirator."

I had been talking to him, telling him different things about his sister, and how he had to get up, get ready for school, and get potty trained. I strongly believe that he was fighting the respirator because he heard me talking to him. He heard his mama's voice.

I had tried to sleep for a couple of hours Saturday night, but I couldn't. I ended up sitting with Benjie while Buster slept in the waiting room. Buster sent me home the next morning at about 7 a.m. after calling and waking David and Diana Pollard. He asked them to come to the hospital and get me so I could go home and change clothes.

When we got to the apartment, Diana Pollard straightened up the living room for me, while I got dressed. She removed all the paramedics' paraphernalia so that Buster wouldn't see it. Then, we went to her mother's house so that I could see Tiffany for a few minutes and reassure her that her mama and daddy had not forgotten her. I was thankful that she was too young to understand what was going on. Benjie's condition was hard enough for us to deal with, without having to comfort or explain things to her too. I held her and talked to her for a little while. Buster wanted me to do that. Then David brought me back to the hospital while Diana stayed at her mother's house with my Tiffany and her three kids. Diana's mother lived between our house and the hospital.

When I got back to the hospital, Buster told me that Benjie's fever had shot up and he'd stopped fighting the respirator. The doctors said it would just be a matter of time before his heart would give out, and he would be totally brain dead, if he wasn't already. Benjie had severe brain damage because it took the paramedics and ER doctors forty-eight minutes to restart his heart. The so-called "golden hour" is only twenty minutes for children. I didn't know that until after the fact. The lack of oxygen resulted in severe brain damage.

I went into his room, and started talking to him again, saying, "Benjie, Mama's here. Mama loves you. I'm back. I'm sorry I had to leave you but Daddy sent me home to get a change of clothes." He started fighting the respirator again, so I know he heard me. Later that day, his kidneys started shutting down. By noon on Sunday, even though I was still hopeful, I started facing reality. In my heart, I knew I was going to lose him, but I had been praying all night that God would grant us a miracle and let him live and be all right. But God chose to ignore my pleas, and I surrendered my son to God's care. Throughout Sunday afternoon and evening, I told Benjie to watch for the light at the end of the tunnel, and to go to the light. Oly was waiting for him on the other side, along with his great-grandparents, Floyd and Linnie Taylor; Grandma Bobbie; and Davey Allison, his favorite race car driver. They would all be waiting to see him.

I finally slept for about six hours that night in the hospital waiting room. Buster was going to send me home, and I said, "Okay, let's go." He said, "I'm not leaving him." I said, "Well, if you're not leaving him, then I'm not leaving him either."

My brother Bill and my nephew Billy had arrived earlier Sunday afternoon, around 1:30 p.m. They joined us in our vigil outside Benjie's room. After a while, they went to the Palace Station Hotel/Casino to spend the night. When they arrived, my friend Paula and I were sitting outside the hospital taking a break. She saw them before I did. We all went upstairs to see Benjie before they left for the hotel.

At around 9 a.m. on Monday morning, August 22, John, the nurse, came to us in the waiting room. He told us that there was a test that they could run on Benjie to see if any blood was getting to the brain. It could only be done at the parents'

request and the test was only done on weekdays. We requested it.

They would take Benjie to the main hospital by special
ambulance and be back by 10 a.m. When they got back they
said that he had fared very well. We learned though that all
hope was lost. The test showed that absolutely no blood was
reaching his brain. The time to decide whether or not to end
life support came to us at 10 a.m. But, Benjie made that decision himself and spared us, his parents. At 10:38 (PDT) his
heart stopped. He made his way to the light at the end of the
tunnel, just like his mama had told him to do, without ever
regaining consciousness.

That little boy, ninety-five percent of the time, would do
what was asked of him. This one time I wish he hadn't been so
well behaved. It was the last unselfish thing that he could do.

Buster and I each held Benjie. I held my little boy for the
last time. He had put up such a fight. The only comfort was
knowing that nothing could ever hurt him again.

Chapter 8

Our Light Goes Out

Benjie had been on life support from the moment he arrived at the hospital to the moment of his death. He had three nurses during his hospital stay, his last a male nurse named John. Numbed by the expected yet sudden death of my son, I walked around the Pediatric Intensive Care Unit like a zombie. I abruptly turned around and found John with Tiffany in his arms. He asked me if I was looking for her, and I said, "No, you go ahead and hold her. I can't right now." He replied, "Thanks, I need to." That statement helped to open my eyes, making me realize how much pain these PICU nurses face everyday. Although Benjie had been one of only a few critical ICU cases in the PICU in quite a while, the nurses were people with feelings, and John was expressing those feelings. Holding onto Benjie's nine-month-old little sister was soothing. Benjie's little sister was alive. Young as she was that day, she would be the catalyst for holding me together in the months to come.

While I was walking around and sometimes talking to the nurses and other parents, my brother, Wilson, and my nephew, Billy, arrived. I had contacted Wilson by phone earlier at their hotel and told him of Benjie's death. Buster was in Benjie's room holding our sweet baby boy's lifeless body in his lap and saying his good-byes, as I had done right after he died. The curtain and the sliding glass door to his room were closed to give us privacy in our grief, and to prevent scaring the other children in the unit. Some were too young to understand the concept of death, but others might be afraid that they would be next.

Buster had left me alone to say good-bye to Benjie, and I did the same for him. I did not return to the room until I was summoned by Buster.

Meanwhile, I talked to the nurses and checked on Tiffany who was doing a lot of "lap hopping." They all loved her and thought that she was a precious little doll. No one could get over how quiet she was. Finding her okay, I took a lot of phone calls at the nurses' station from friends and family all over the country. Then, I faced the hardest task of all. I had to call my parents and tell them that the battle was over and that death had taken their favorite grandchild. After I got off the phone with my mom, I went back into Benjie's room to find Buster talking with a representative of the Clark County, Nevada, coroner's office. We filled out the information forms needed for the death certificate, as well as the paperwork required to release Benjie's body for burial in California. We stipulated on those forms that we didn't want an autopsy. We saw him write: "Parents demand NO AUTOPSY." Nothing would be learned from an autopsy. There was nothing to learn, and he had been under a doctor's care at the time of his death. Buster and I thought an autopsy would be pointless, and we didn't want them to cut up his otherwise perfect little body. The representative assured us that no autopsy would be done, and, after shaking our hands and expressing his sympathy, he left.

We said our last hospital good-byes to Benjie. It was so difficult to kiss a lifeless forehead and say good-bye. I had never in his life said good-bye to him. I always said, "see you later," or "be back soon, I love you," or "be a good boy, I love you," but never good-bye. This time he couldn't hear me, let alone respond.

I literally had to be pulled away from his bedside. I couldn't bear the thought of strangers even touching my little boy. I kept thinking, "He'll be scared. I have to stay with him because he'll be scared if I'm not there." I could hear his little voice yelling, "I want my Mama," but it was just my imagination. I kept wondering as I still do, if he was scared when he went to that light since I wasn't there holding his hand. God knows that I wanted to be with him, making sure my little boy wasn't scared. But I couldn't be. Did he recognize anybody there? Would they know who he was?

With tears streaming down my face, I turned my back on my little boy and walked out of his hospital room. Then, I turned to John, his last nurse, and said, "Thank you for taking such good care of our little boy and would you please convey our thanks to the other nurses that shared those duties." He said that he would, and expressed his condolences with tears in his eyes.

I didn't know it then, but it would be four days before I would see my little boy's face again. The longest that I had ever been away from Benjie was overnight, ten months ago when I gave birth to Tiffany.

Buster, Tiffany, Wilson, Billy, and I got on the elevator and
quietly went downstairs. As we got to the entrance of the
building, Buster, who had been carrying Tiffany in her carrier,
set her down, turned to me, and asked if I wanted to have
another child. The question caught me off guard, and I replied
with the first thing that came into my mind. "It wouldn't be
fair to the child." What's more, we both agreed, it wouldn't
bring Benjie back, nor was there any guarantee the child would
be a boy, and, most of all, no child could take Benjie's place in
our hearts or our lives. No, I decided, I had carried two children, and for ten months I had my perfect family. I didn't want
any more children.

Buster picked up Tiffany again, and we went outside into
the blistering heat of that Las Vegas day. We walked for what
seemed like forever until we came to my brother's black Ford
Explorer. It was a quiet ride back to our apartment. We only
spoke to give directions to our apartment.

My brother parked at the curb in front of our apartment.
As we got out of the car, a neighbor walked by. I recognized
her from the laundry room. She asked why I looked so upset,
and I told her the news. She expressed her sympathy and then
continued walking as we went up the stairs to our apartment.

We went in and turned on the lights. Everything was basically the way we had left it. Benjie's glass of tea was still sitting
on the kitchen table. His toy ambulance was still in the living
room where he had left it. I quickly put these things away.
However, I couldn't bring myself to empty the tea that
remained in the cup. I just put it on the kitchen counter and left
it. I kept thinking that he would be back to look for it and
would be upset to find it empty.

The chore of calling people to let them know that the battle was over and we had lost came next. While Wilson and Billy sat on our living room sofa in silence, Buster and I made phone calls. We called my parents first to let them know that we were home. Buster called his brother at work, but he was out on a job. Then, we called Buster's sister in Missouri. Her husband answered the phone. When she and her kids heard the news, I heard crying in the background. Their oldest son's name is also Benjamin, and the two Benjamins were wild about each other.

We had "call waiting" so the phone wasn't ringing constantly. Many people called to find out about Benjie. They wanted to know if the funeral would be in California or Nevada. I even called the local NBC affiliate, KVBC, to let them know what had happened since I had seen one of their cameramen on the street by the ambulance two nights before. I asked for one of their female reporters, but I was told that she was busy on another assignment. They said they would send someone else with a cameraman, if I didn't mind. The name of the reporter was not familiar to me, but Buster and I thought that Benjie would want us to explain what had happened to him so I prepared a brief statement to read on the air. I was told that the reporter would be at our house by 3 p.m.

Before the reporter and his cameraman arrived, Buster disappeared, and no one knew where he was. I had to find my husband. I looked in every room, and finally found him in our bedroom closet. He was sitting quietly on the floor holding baby mementos that I kept in a shoebox. They were Benjie's, and as he looked at each one, he sobbed. My heart broke all over again to see my husband in this state. I begged him to stop torturing himself. I asked him to come into the living room to help me prepare for the reporter's arrival.

A short time later, the reporter was at our door. Billy answered the door for me, and as it opened I exclaimed, "JACK FINN!!!," as he came into the apartment.

We gave Jack a brief history of what had happened that day, and while the cameraman taped us, Jack asked me questions. Then, Buster, Jack, and the cameraman went into the bedroom. We saw the taped news broadcast a week later, and I learned what had transpired. I couldn't bring myself to enter that room again that day. My little boy had virtually died in that room.

Our story was on the 6 o'clock news and the 11 o'clock news that Monday night. Our story followed the lead story. Someone told me earlier that day on the phone that I was being noble for telling our story. I didn't do it to be noble. I did it to warn other parents of the dangers of vertical-blind, mini-blind cords in their homes. After that day, a lot of people that I encountered in stores told me that they either cut the cords, put them out of reach, or just got rid of them altogether. When I told them what had happened to us, they couldn't believe their ears.

That afternoon, the neighbor we had seen on the street as we arrived home stopped by. She came to offer her help, in any way she could. She gave me her phone number and told me to call for anything, at any time. I said, "I'll certainly think about it. Thank you." She told me, "Don't think about it. Do it." Her forcefulness took me a bit by surprise, but we would later be very grateful for her help. Her resemblance to my sister-in-law, Brenda, Buster's sister in Missouri, was uncanny. After telling her that I didn't know what I was planning yet, she left, but only after I promised to call her for anything.

As she was leaving, Paula arrived with the things I had

asked her to bring me when I called her from the hospital. She had apparently picked them up at the apartment that morning instead of waiting until the afternoon. She came with a friend whom I had never met. I was still in shock, but felt a little put out just the same. Later on, I realized how much I resented that Paula had brought a stranger into my house that day. Standing in my living room was a stranger who, I felt, was invading my home in my time of grief. Was I supposed to entertain her? We were in mourning, and there was a stranger in my home. It didn't seem right to have her sitting in my living room and laughing with my brother. However, it was good to see my brother laughing again, reminiscing about his childhood. Billy, Bill, Paula, and the stranger visited and laughed, while Buster and I continued packing. Tiffany lay in her playpen, out of the way and safe.

Buster disappeared again, and I went to look for him. This time I found him behind closed doors in Benjie's room. He was in Benjie's closet and again sobbing his heart out. He was looking for an outfit in which to bury our son. He finally decided on one, and I wholeheartedly agreed that the most appropriate outfit was Benjie's Teenage Mutant Ninja Turtle outfit, complete with red headband. He had worn it for Halloween the previous year in San Diego. He was so proud of that outfit. He had worn it several times since Halloween. If I had let him, he would have lived in it. He loved it so much, and he looked so cute in it.

Buster put the two-piece outfit, the turtle sox and underpants, the red headband, and a turtle figurine and communicator in a shoebox. He did it so that I wouldn't have to face it. I hadn't even begun to think about such details. I was just barely functioning.

He started packing Benjie's things that night so that we wouldn't have that much to do when we got back. We packed enough for a week, so by the time we left for California that night around sundown, the car trunk was full. The backseat was stuffed, and the front floor was so full I didn't have much legroom. What didn't fit in our car, Bill and Billy took in theirs. It was so weird to make that trip without Benjie in the car with us. He had always sat in the backseat with me whenever we traveled. Now, we were a family of three, all stuffed in the front seat.

I hadn't known until 5 p.m. that afternoon that Bill wanted to go back home that night. He had to get back to his office. Buster couldn't bring himself to sleep in the apartment, let alone that bedroom, and I knew that I couldn't either.

As the four people in the living room continued to visit, I gathered the things I wanted to have with me for the week. We were going to stay at my parents' house in Tustin. We arrived there around 1:30 a.m. Tuesday morning, August 23, 1994.

Before we left, Buster and I had discussed which day would be best for Benjie's burial. We couldn't bring ourselves to have it on Friday, August 26, because on that day Tiffany would be ten months old. We couldn't have it on Monday, August 29, because that day marked the month before his fourth birthday. We decided to bury Benjie on Saturday, August 27, because he had been born on a Saturday, and that's what we did.

Chapter 9

Choosing His Eternal Bed

On Monday, August 22, 1994, I had called Jim Kane of Saddleback Chapel from Las Vegas. After about six hours sleep Monday night, I got up quietly, trying not to awaken Buster or Tiffany. Later that morning, the phone rang. Jim Kane was on the other end. He told me that there was a holdup in getting Benjie out of Las Vegas. The hospital had informed the coroner's office that we had approved the "harvest" of Benjie's organs. Hearing that, I screamed, "No!" into the phone and handed the cordless phone to Buster. He had to hear it from Jim as I had. Through sobs, I told my parents what had happened.

I had never seen my father cry before. While holding me, this seventy-nine-year-old man was crying because he knew that the hospital's mistake was torture for me. The mental anguish alone was almost unbearable. I felt like my baby's body was being held for ransom. They would release him only if we surrendered his organs. What right did the hospital have to overrule us? We hadn't signed any release forms allowing them to do anything but release his whole body to the coroner's office so that they could transport it to the local mortuary. There it would be prepared for travel to Saddleback Chapel where all further arrangements were to be made.

A few minutes later, Buster got off the phone. Jim Kane had informed Buster that, due to a federal law, an autopsy would have to be performed on Benjie's body. Two cuts would be made—one down the back of his skull and one down the middle of his back. The cuts would not be visible at the viewing, and we wouldn't know they were there. I said, "I'll know." That's what hurt. We sat down and Buster held me as I cried some more.

Jim Kane told Buster that we would have to get a cemetery plot before we could arrange for burial. Meantime, he would call the Las Vegas hospital back to inform them of their error and secure Benjie's release.

We got dressed and went to the Santa Ana Cemetery on Santa Clara Avenue, to discuss purchasing a plot for our son. It was rather difficult for me, so Buster did most of the talking. Basically, I just sat and listened, nodding in agreement whenever I could.

It was a hot day in Santa Ana. We walked from the office to the area where we would have to choose a plot for Benjie. I was carrying Tiffany in my arms, and, having short legs, I had trouble keeping up with the two men ahead of me. Mostly though, I lagged behind because I didn't want to be at a cemetery picking out a plot for my dead son. My heart ached.

When I finally got to the area that was designated as still open, Buster asked if I wanted to lay Benjie between the two trees near the green pump house. He would be easy to find in years to come, especially if we moved away and came back to visit him. We wouldn't forget that space. I said, "That would be fine," and we went back to the office to make the final financial arrangements for the plot. At that time, we were given the option of purchasing two adjacent plots to Benjie's for ourselves. I would be at his head with his daddy to my right. A few weeks later, we took that option so that we may be together again with our son.

Later, we went home and got together with my folks and told them of the morning's accomplishments. Then, we called Jim Kane at Saddleback Chapel and made arrangements to meet with him the next day to make final arrangements for Benjie's funeral and burial.

Jim Kane had learned that two Benjamins had been at the coroner's office in Las Vegas. The other Benjamin had been killed in a drive-by shooting, and autopsy would have to be performed on him in order to retrieve the bullet for forensics and future legal action.

That phone call relieved our fears that our wishes for our son's body were going to be respected. We would receive him whole, as he had been born.

Chapter 10

Making Arrangements

I awoke that Wednesday morning contemplating the events the day would bring. I got dressed and I was as ready as I could be emotionally for what I had to face later that day.

We sat with Jim Kane in his office at Saddleback Mortuary chapel for the better part of a couple of hours, making all the arrangements for Benjie's final resting place. I had thought it would take about half an hour.

Although Benjie was still in Las Vegas, a transport truck was heading that way to pick him up and bring him back to California. He would be prepared for burial and dressed in his "turtle outfit," with all its accessories, at Saddleback Chapel.

Meantime, Jim, Buster, and I went through each arrangement in detail for Benjie's funeral. We were advised of the financial charges. We were grateful to Jim for keeping costs as low as possible. The emotional hardship of burying our son was hard enough.

After establishing which clothes would be put on our son's body for his burial, we went on to "design" the funeral program. I had written our son's eulogy and used some of it in the program. Buster and I both wanted everyone to know what kind of child our son had been. His picture would be on the front cover of the program, along with his name and the dates of his birth and death. Clouds would adorn the background of the program, which to me depicted the heavens in such a serene manner.

Inside the program was a poem we had chosen from a book we found at Saddleback Chapel. Also inside the program was another picture of our son with a big smile on his face. I remember the day that picture was taken. It was shortly after the birth of his sister, and in those days he always had a smile on his face. The poem we had chosen, "God Loves Children," was underneath that photograph. At the bottom of the facing page was part of the eulogy I had written. It read:

Benjamin was our little angel here on earth. He was a sensitive, loving little boy who was full of personality, adored his little sister, idolized his cousins and loved his parents and grandparents. We feel blessed to have been his parents.

All who knew him loved him. He touched so many lives during his short time with us, whether they were friends or strangers.

We love you Benjie and we will all be together again someday in God's open arms.

Above that was the customary information—his name and nickname were at the top, followed by his birth date and birthplace, and the date and place of death, the date, time, and location of the service. The officiant, the eulogist, and the names of the pallbearers and the location of his final resting place were also on the program.

We felt it fitting that the man who had married us and baptized both Benjie and his sister should guide us through this difficult time. We wanted Richard Irving of the First Congregational Church of Santa Ana, California, to help us bury our son. He agreed without a moment of hesitation. I had been in touch with him while we were at the hospital. He had been a very comforting voice to me, especially in the hours I was waiting for Buster to arrive on that first night.

I would deliver the eulogy, since I felt I was the one who truly knew and understood our son. Also, it was the last opportunity I would have to do some "bragging" about what a good boy and special person he was.

After completing the program design and giving all the information needed, Buster and I had the difficult task of selecting a casket for our son's body. I knew from the previous experiences of friends what to expect. The room full of nothing but caskets did not come as a surprise. However, I wasn't prepared for the emotional impact of choosing the one that would contain my son's remains for eternity. That decision proved to be very difficult, as I'm sure any loving person can well imagine, if they don't actually know from firsthand experience.

We were directed to some small, white, child-sized caskets. Some were adorned in fabric and lace, and others were just painted. We chose a painted casket for Benjie. Since he measured forty-two inches at the time of his death, it was initially planned that the size of his casket would be that length also. I took one look at that casket, and told the person helping us that it would be too small for my son's body. We would need a casket measuring no less than four feet long. I turned out to be correct. The casket had a beautiful little white satinlike pillow on which his small head would rest.

I finally had to leave the room and go back to Jim's office. Emotionally, I couldn't take the pain any longer. It was too difficult for me to be in that room, knowing that my little boy would, in a few days, be placed in that box and buried, and people would walk on the ground covering him.

While we were in the casket room, Tiffany had quietly remained in her car carrier in Jim Kane's office. She even managed to nap for a brief period after she finished her bottle. I stayed with her, waiting for Jim Kane and Buster to return from the casket room. When they returned to Jim's office, we finished discussing the details of all the arrangements, including the possibility of having a bagpiper at the service.

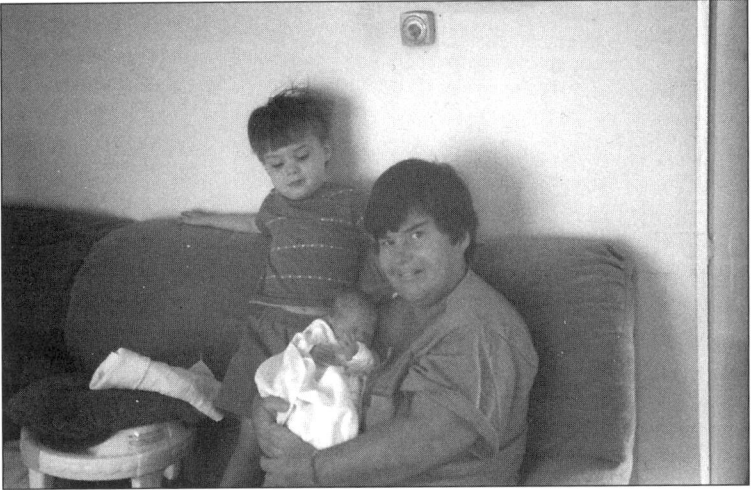

This was the day after Tiffany's birth, with big brother looking out for his little sister.

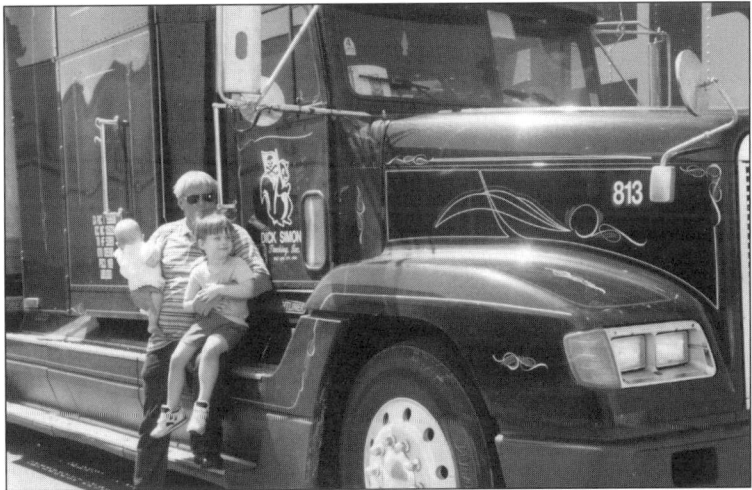

My family outside the truck Buster was driving that fateful night.

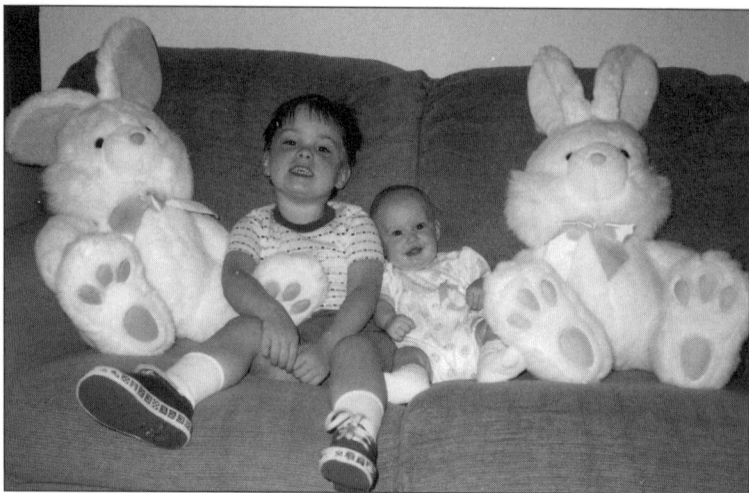

My folks gave the bunnies to the kids for Easter in 1994. It was also Benjie's last one.

This is our family on one of our many visits to the grave.

The building in which our son died.

BENJAMIN LEE TAYLOR
"BENJIE"
SEPT. 29, 1990   AUG. 22, 1994
DADDY'S LITTLE BUDDY — MAMA'S LITTLE BOY

Our son today.

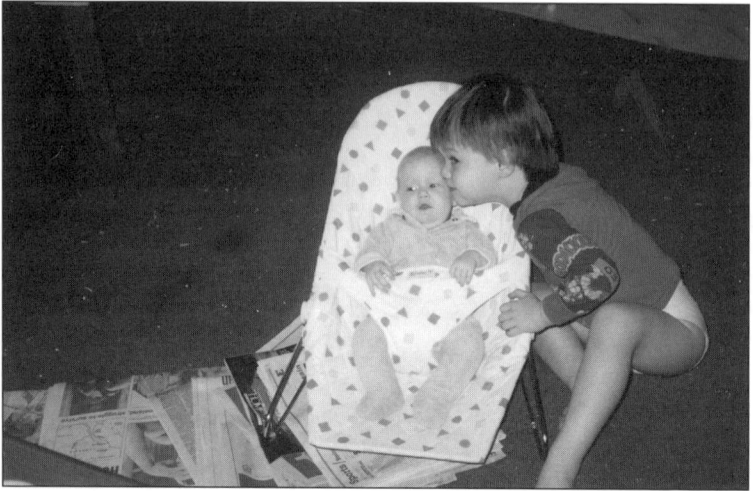

Benjamin and Tiffany share a tender moment.

This is the last picture I ever took of my son. Ironically, it was his idea. This photo is in every home in our family.

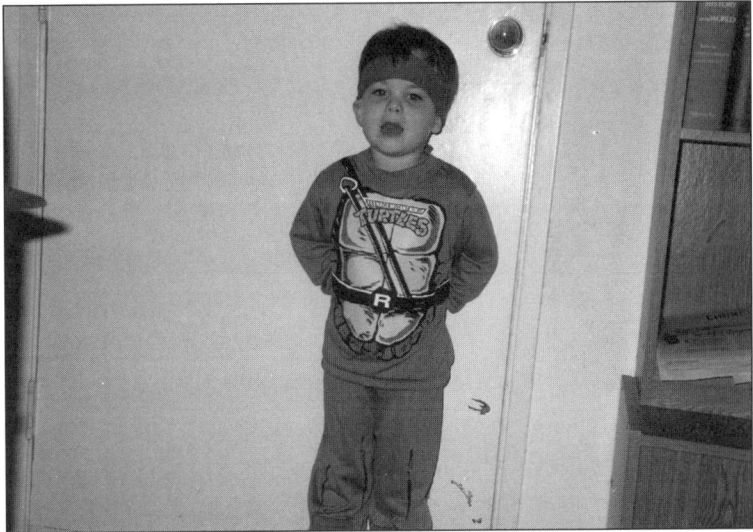

Here is Benjie in his costume for Halloween in 1993. We buried him in this outfit.

Tiffany — 6 years old.

Chapter II

Spreading the Word

Thursday morning it was bright and sunny outside, but not in our hearts, as we prepared ourselves and Tiffany for the long drive south to San Diego. The task that lay ahead would not be easy, but, then, there was nothing easy about that entire week.

Even though we had moved away from the area, we still had a lot of friends there, and they had to be told of Benjie's death. They shouldn't be told by phone and we needed a break. I wanted to go, visit, and get away from the painful events of the week, if only for a second.

When we arrived near our old apartment, we went into the grocery store where Benjie had made himself and his good manners known every time he politely asked for a cookie at the bakery window. The girl behind the counter immediately asked me where he was, and I had to tell her the news. She told her co-workers and they were as shocked as she was. When our favorite cashier, Mike, came back from his break, we told him. I remember saying, "Mike, we lost Benjie." He replied, "What do you mean, you lost him?" I said, "He's dead." He stopped what he was doing and turned to me with a look of complete shock on his face. He said the same thing I had been hearing from everyone all week long. What? How? When? Where? He immediately embraced me, and I told him briefly what had happened, because I didn't want to interfere with his duties. Promising to keep in touch, we left for our next destination, the local Target store, to tell the tragic news to our many friends who worked there. We went to each and every place as planned, including our former doctor's office. He had known Benjie since even before his birth, but he was on vacation that week, and we missed him. We did tell the nurse and the receptionist, and they were shocked and sad to hear the news. They both told me what a cute little guy he had been, and, being his mother, I couldn't have agreed more.

After eating lunch at one of our local hangouts, we went to the apartment complex to see our former neighbors and tell them the news. Not many people were home in the middle of the day. But some had moved into homes of their own and were still in the area so we went to see them. We talked with them for a short time before making the long drive home to Tustin.

We had driven almost two hundred miles that day and we were tired and emotionally drained. I couldn't eat as my nerves were still shot, and my stomach was upset.

We called Jim Kane at Saddleback Chapel and learned that Benjie's body had arrived safely and was being prepared for viewing the next day.

Chapter 12

Saying Our Good-byes

We decided to have a quiet, private family viewing of Benjie the evening before the funeral. The day before the funeral was also a time to try to catch our breath and gather our strength for what the following days would bring.

I had arranged to have my hair cut by my mom's hairdresser. She's a sweet Japanese woman who had done my mom's hair for years. After she finished with my mom's hair, she cut mine. She had been very fond of Benjie and was very upset by his death. He had been very fond of her, too.

Buster had gone out to the store for some soda, but he had been gone for a long time. When he got home, he told us that he had stopped by Saddleback Chapel, and picked up some copies of the program to show me. He also saw our son. The people at Saddleback thoughtfully reassured Buster that no cuts had been made on our son's body, and showed him Benjie's back and head. Buster warned me that seeing Benjie would be very difficult for me, but he thought that Benjie looked very good, that they had captured his personality by the way they made up his face. Everyone who worked there had been affected by the little boy and the tragic way in which he died.

Jim Kane had told Buster that he had located a bagpiper who was willing to play at the service. He would play "Amazing Grace" on the bagpipes. Our son loved bagpipe music as much as we do. I am mostly Scottish and Buster is one-quarter, which gave Benjie his appreciation for the music.

I took one look at the advance copy of the funeral program, with Benjie's picture on the front cover, that Buster had been given and broke down. I wanted to see my little boy again, laughing with his daddy and playing with his sister, instead of on the front cover of a funeral program. I dreaded the approaching evening and having to say good-bye for the last time to my son, my miracle baby, my little ray of sunshine.

We had asked that our minister, Reverend Richard Irving, be in attendance with the family at the viewing. He had come to the house earlier in the week to discuss the selection of hymns and details of the service. He also took care of getting an organist from his church.

We arrived at Saddleback Chapel just before viewing time. We found my sister-in-law Allison there, sobbing. She had come from work and had already seen Benjie. Buster took my hand and slowly led me to the other side of the room where our son's open casket was resting. As I approached it, I kept saying to myself, "Please God, let me wake up from this horrible dream. This isn't really happening." But it was. I was surprised to see that Buster had been right about how well they had prepared Benjie. He looked like a little mannequin lying there, almost too perfect. He was so cute, dressed in his turtle outfit. He had a towel covering him like a blanket. He held his turtle communicator in one hand and a turtle action figure in the other, and the red headband was around his perfect little head. "Buddy," the stuffed version of the lead turtle known as Leonardo, was sitting at his feet "watching" over him. Bill and Allison gave Benjie that toy for his second birthday. Benjie never went anywhere without Buddy and we decided that he would never be separated from Buddy. We would bury Buddy with our son.

Buster was right again. Seeing Benjie was very difficult for me. I needed a chair so that I could sit next to my son and look down on his angelic little face for the last time. He was so cold, and I just wanted to pick him up and warm him with my body, but I couldn't. I couldn't do anything for him ever again. I could only sit and cry. It had been four days since I had last seen my son's beautiful little face. This would be the last time I would see his face in the flesh.

Eventually, Buster led me away so that other family members could see Benjie. I took a chair close by and talked with Richard Irving about the events of the following day, and other things to try to distract myself from any thoughts of any kind in my head. We talked about anything and everything, including the weather.

My father helped my mother walk to the casket, as she was using a walker. It proved to be almost more than she could handle but she did it. It still had not sunk in with any of us that this was really happening. It was all just a big mistake. That wasn't my son lying in that box. It had to be someone else's unfortunate hardship and heartbreak. There are times even now, six years later, that I can't believe he is dead, I can't bring myself to believe it. Then I go to the cemetery and look at the headstone and it hits me like a ton of bricks all over again.

Each family member in turn went to our son's side for one last time. My brother was with us, as he had been in Las Vegas. My sister and my brother-in-law were the only family members not in attendance that evening. My brother-in-law had been out of town all week and was due home late that evening. He and my sister would, however, be at the funeral the next day. They lived in the next county, which is an hour's drive from the chapel.

Finally, it was Tiffany's turn to say good-bye to her big brother one last time. Buster took her from Allison, who had been holding her for me, and carried her to Benjie's side. I remember how she looked down on his face, and the bewildered look that came over her tiny face. She was only ten months old, and we were asking her to do what we were having difficulty doing ourselves. She would look at Benjie, then over her daddy's shoulder at the rest of the family and then back to Benjie. She did this "circuit" several times. I felt my heart breaking all over again for what I believed was going through our daughter's young mind. The only thought that came into mine was, "How come he's not talking to me? How come he doesn't open his eyes and say something?"

Ever since the first time he saw her, after her birth in the hospital, Benjie had never failed to talk to her. He was always at her side. I could not keep him away from her. He was totally devoted to his sister and her every need. He was hurt if we didn't let him feed, bathe, play with, or touch her. The only chore he gladly surrendered was changing her diapers, and he was only three years older than Tiffany. Twice, I had caught him in her playpen with her simply because he wanted to be as close to her as he could.

Finally, it was time to leave the building and say good-bye. I kissed his cold forehead, and, with a heavy heart, reluctantly left. I walked to the car and we left for the short ride home. Saturday, August 27, 1994, 1 p.m. would come soon enough.

Chapter 13

The Funeral

I had been working on the eulogy over the past week, and it was finally polished for today. I made a silent promise to Benjie that I would get through my delivery without breaking down. It was a difficult promise to keep, but I did keep it.

In the eulogy, I described some cute incidents that had taken place between Benjie and me. One of them occurred shortly before I found him in our bedroom that last time. He was always coming up with new ideas, words that really kept us on our toes and taught us so many things. He reminded us of the things that we, as adults, sometimes took for granted.

The funeral was scheduled for 1 p.m. It was a busy morning, with everyone asking me what they should wear. I had already told everyone to wear clothes in which Benjie would recognize them. I would be wearing black pants and a purple pullover blouse; I wanted my son to know that I was there, and not looking like a stranger. I didn't particularly want the men

in suits and ties. I just wanted them to come in relaxed cloth-
ing, since Benjie had seldom seen them in suits. Buster wore a
tie but no jacket.

It was a hot and humid August day, but I didn't notice. My
nerves were still raw. I was still acclimated to the Las Vegas
heat, and the wet heat of Southern California didn't have much
effect. Actually, the heat felt good, since I felt very cold.

We had received cards, letters, phone calls, and flowers
from all our friends and family around the country. One of my
closest friends called in tears when she heard the news. She
and I had not been able to keep in touch for a few years, and
the bad news came as quite a shock to her. She had thrown the
baby shower for me when Benjie was six weeks old. She told
me that she would definitely be at the funeral to support me in
any way that she could.

My cousin, Diane, whom I had never met, came for the
funeral. Another friend came all the way from Omaha,
Nebraska. Having boys of their own and compassion in their
hearts, they felt they should be at my side. The friends who
had been in our wedding party stood at our sides during the
service. Some of our San Diego friends, whose children Benjie
had played with, came to say their good-byes. Among them
was a friend who had just visited us three months earlier in
Las Vegas.

The car for the family arrived at 12:15 p.m. I was barely
ready, having just gotten Tiffany dressed and ready to go. My
mom sat in the front seat with the driver, since that was the
easiest seat for her to take. My father sat in the middle, and
Buster, Tiffany, and I took the seats in the back of the car. It was
a black limousine; I had always wondered what they looked
like on the inside, but I never wanted to find out this way. The

driver was a very nice older man, who treated me with great compassion and respect. He seemed to have been touched by our loss.

The drive to the cemetery's chapel was short. As we pulled into the side entrance, reserved for family members, we saw the hearse containing our son's body parked in front of the chapel. When I walked in, a woman approached, calling me by name, and was about to identify herself when I said, "Diane, I'd know those Hart eyes anywhere." She is the daughter of my father's brother, therefore we share the same maiden name. We embraced and proceeded into the family's room adjacent to the chapel, where I introduced her to Buster. The family members talked for a few minutes, but my attention was drawn to the back of the church. Benjie's casket was sitting on a wheeled platform waiting for the pallbearers to bring it to the front of the chapel.

I walked over and put my hand on Benjie's casket before turning to friends nearby. I talked to an attorney with whom I had worked, and his wife, who was gracious enough to attend the service. He met Benjie on several occasions when I visited the office while I was in town. The other members of the office staff had been unable to make the service, but had sent their condolences. I thanked them for coming and returned to the front of the room to join the rest of my family.

A few minutes later, I heard someone sobbing. I turned around and saw Buster leading the close friend whom I had not seen for a long time toward me. She was beside herself with grief for me and for Benjie. She was the friend who had given us the wonderful baby shower, and she had also been my matron of honor. Having a small son of her own, she could well imagine our pain.

To look at the two of us, someone might have thought that she was the bereaved parent rather than me, since I was the one consoling her and trying to calm her down. It shows the depth of my friends' love and compassion for me, and I thank each and every one of them from the bottom of my heart.

The service was about to begin. The pallbearers wheeled Benjie's casket to the front of the church. Three of them were family members. The fourth had been in our wedding party, as well as his wife. His wife and I grew up together and had known each other for almost thirty-five years.

Reverend Richard Irving began the service with an introductory and a prayer. I took the podium for the eulogy, which I think surprised a lot of people. I saw many familiar faces, including many of the parents who had been my neighbors while growing up on Lambeth Way in Tustin. Now, they were helping me say good-bye to my little boy.

As nervous as I was about speaking before an audience, I felt more at ease than I had ever felt before. I was in front of friends and family, people who had known me for most of my life and who had been with me through some of my darkest moments. They had been there when Buster and I got married. Why should I be nervous? I was there to speak about Benjie's life. I had promised Benjie I would get through his eulogy without breaking down, and I didn't—until after I had delivered the last line, saying, "Thank you for loving our little boy."

After I spoke, Buster said a few words. Then he helped me, his sobbing wife, walk past our son's small white casket. We went back to the family's room where he held me while I cried even harder for the rest of the service.

The church service concluded and I thought we would be leaving, but one of the men from Saddleback Chapel, who had been with Benjie since his arrival in California, approached Buster. He asked if we would agree to open the casket and allow the mourners to pay their last respects. After a slight pause during which Buster and I considered, we agreed, and people lined up to see his sweet, innocent face once more.

At this point, my nephew Billy and his three sisters, then eleven, ten and seven years old, got scared. My brother knelt down in front of them, telling them to remember Benjie the way he had been. He didn't want his children to see Benjie now. It was not easy for us and he was afraid it would be a never-ending nightmare for the children. They had not even suffered the loss of a pet, yet here they were at the funeral of a cousin younger than the youngest of them. Their hearts were full of enough pain, and their eyes were full of tears. We didn't want to add to their pain. What purpose would it serve to subject them to it?

During my delivery of the eulogy, I had not really looked out at everyone in the audience. I was touched by the faces that now approached me after walking past my son's casket. My mom's hairdresser and her husband; the owner, head waitress, and busboy from our favorite Mexican restaurant; the nurse and receptionist from my former doctor's office; all were there.

After the last person paid his condolences, it was time to leave for the graveside service. As they were closing Benjie's casket, I stopped them. I had Tiffany in my arms, and I wanted her to have one more chance to see her brother's face. I kissed his forehead one more time, then I gave Tiffany to my sister-in-law, who was looking after Tiffany for me that day.

We went out to the car, and I asked Diane to come with us in the family car. I wanted to talk with her and get to know her better. The hearse was parked in front of the family car, and I watched the men load my son's body into it for the short drive through the cemetery to the grave site. As we got out of the car, I saw the chairs lined up alongside the hole in the ground. The chairs were draped in green material, and there was a green canopy overhead. Buster took the first chair, and I sat next to him. Allison sat next to me with Tiffany, followed by the three kids, their mother, and my sister. Everyone else was invited to gather around behind us. Once again, my friends rallied behind me. Buster and I felt hands on our shoulders. Buster held one of my hands, and, with the other one, I held the hand of a friend. Tiffany was as quiet as a mouse, content in being close to her parents.

I was fine during this portion of the service, until the bagpiper began playing "Amazing Grace." It was the hymn that we had chosen and it was beautiful, yet painful. Benjie shared my love for bagpipe music and I wanted our son to hear it just one more time.

Soon the service was over, and it was time to leave. This was it, the FINAL time, the moment I had been dreading. I had to turn my back on my son and walk away, but I couldn't get up. I swore to Benjie at his grave that someone would pay for his death, someone would be made to answer for why my little boy was taken from us at such an early age. The anger I felt was almost as overwhelming as the heartache. That rage got me through the rest of the day.

Buster pleaded with me to leave the cemetery. He wanted to stay and watch them lower our son's casket into the ground and cover it with all the flowers that surrounded it. I asked him why I couldn't stay too. Benjie was just as much my son as he was his. He said that someone had to be at the house to greet our guests who would be coming to pay their personal respects. That someone would have to be me as Tiffany was too young for the job. My brother offered to stay with Buster and bring him home.

Buster thanked the bagpiper for his musical services. The man said that if he had known that the service was for a small child, he would have asked at least four other bagpipers to play for no additional charge.

We sat in the car for a few minutes before leaving. The driver asked me if I wanted to leave, and after a brief pause, I said, "Let's go." I said a silent good-bye to my son as the car left the curb.

Back at the house, I got together with all my friends and talked, and yes, even laughed, about the good times we had shared. Most of us knew each other from high school or earlier and we had a lot of catching up to do.

Buster and my brother appeared about an hour later. They had waited in the shade of a nearby tree, out of the heat of the day, for the groundskeepers to tend to Benjie's burial. Then, Buster and Bill placed the flowers on the grave themselves.

I ate, for one of the first times in a while. However, I would later regret it, since my nerves and intestines would wage war on my body.

Finally, it was only the family again, and we sat and talked about the day's events and the friends with whom we had shared them. I was emotionally and physically exhausted. For the first time in a week, I would sleep through the night.

Chapter 14

The Future

On August 29, we packed a few things that we would need for a short trip and left for the apartment in Las Vegas. We were going there to pack the rest of our belongings and move back to California permanently. Buster said that he didn't want to worry about his remaining family while he was on the road. We would move back into my childhood home and live with my parents until we found an affordable place of our own.

The neighbor who had given me her phone number and asked me to call if I needed any help was the first person I called when we got home. I also called Paula, the friend who had helped us get the Las Vegas apartment. She offered to help me pack that week after work and on her days off.

I packed with help from the girls, getting rid of a lot of junk that I didn't want any more. I also gave some of Benjie's things to the neighbors' kids as mementos of their friendship. Buster kept us supplied with boxes, and he lined up the movers. We worked day and night and got the job done in three days. At night, the three of us slept in the living room on the mattress from Tiffany's room. I couldn't go into our bedroom again, and Buster knew it.

After writing a note to the apartment complex office explaining our intention to move, we scheduled the movers for Friday, September 2, 1994. The living room furniture was the last to go, so we had that to rest on while the movers took our things from the bedrooms. There were moments that were almost impossible for me to handle emotionally. Benjie's wagon was accidentally left in front of me in the living room, while the movers took other things down to the truck. I had to hide my eyes, and Paula, told me when it was gone so that I could look up again. Benjie had loved that wagon and was waiting for the day when he could take his little sister out for a ride in it.

The movers had heard about Benjie's death on the news and were surprised to find that we were his parents. We were the most well-known family in the area during that time. If anyone heard our name or our story, they instantly knew who we were.

The moving van left with our things that afternoon. We packed the car with the rest of our odds and ends, and spent the night in a motel on the outskirts of Las Vegas. It was strange to be in the car without Benjie. We all sat in the front seat, since the rest of the car, as well as the trunk, was stuffed with our belongings.

We settled into the motel room for the night, or at least we tried to; Tiffany would not stop crying. We had left her stuffed toy in the car. Benjie had given her that toy in July, and she held onto it from then on. I remember saying that he should keep it because she wouldn't know the difference. He replied, "I'll know the difference, Mama." He wanted his sister to have it. It was a fluffy white chimp holding a banana. Buster got up, dressed, and went to the car to get the toy chimp. As soon as Tiffany got her hands on it, she started to settle down. Minutes later, she was fast asleep. A couple of hours later, we followed her example.

The next morning we left Nevada. I never wanted to see the state again. Much more precious than my shirt, I had lost my son in this state.

Our furniture arrived on Tuesday, September 6, the day after Labor Day. During our week in Tustin before the funeral, we had made arrangements to have our things put into a local storage lot. Our furniture was unpacked and put into storage, and later at the house, the remaining items we needed to have there were unloaded. We prepared to go on with our lives without Benjie. However, he would live on in our hearts.

Chapter 15

TCF Help

Since I had received psychological counseling in the past, Buster urged me to seek it out again in order to help me find peace in my grief. At his request, I called my counselor, who gave me names of support groups, which he thought would better serve my needs. I called a few and finally settled on one called "The Compassionate Friends." I later learned that there are chapters of this organization all over the world, with over 600 chapters in the United States alone.

I attended my first meeting on September 21, 1994, the night before the one month anniversary of Benjie's death. I took a photo of Benjie and Tiffany, the last one taken of my kids together. My tears flowed, but I got my story out. I was allowed to cry, yell, do whatever I needed at the time without anyone telling me that I was doing something wrong. I got support from other bereaved parents, as I, in turn, would later support newly bereaved parents as they confronted their grief. Since then, I have joined a re-established chapter in my area, and I did the monthly newsletter for a while.

The Compassionate Friends, or TCF, as it is referred to by its members, was started in 1969 by an English chaplain who brought two couples together after the deaths of their two children. The couples got together to console each other. Who could better understand their grief than someone who has "been there?"

It's surprising how many people don't want you to talk about your child, and that hurts. They want you to get over it and get on with your life. When a child dies, it's not like losing a pet. You cannot "replace" a child. When a child dies, he is not forgotten. Benjie will always be a part of our family. No one will every change that. We have gone on with our lives. We have to for Tiffany's sake. However, Benjie's mom, as he knew her, is gone. Tiffany's mom is here for her. I have the right to see at least one of my children grow up. That child is Tiffany.

I still need the support of The Compassionate Friends. That may change but for now, I've got friends within the "Friends." Because of my son's death, I have made new friends, and we all have one very strong bond—the love for our children.

Being the newsletter editor for my TCF chapter has proven to be both beneficial and very rewarding to me in ways that I can't begin to describe. Knowing that I brought a little happiness, relief, understanding, or hope into another bereaved parent's day makes my healing that much stronger. Of course, I still have days when I can't stop the tears, but then there are days when I'll get a phone call from someone who needs me to listen. I'll do my best to be there for that person, just as someone else will be there for me when I need to talk.

I've done a lot of writing since Benjie died, and have quite a collection of poems, articles, letters and quotes that help me to convey my feelings. I have been able to use some of my creative "juices," and have acquired new hobbies or gone back to old ones. I never enjoyed writing in school, but then I wrote because I had to, not because I wanted to do it. Writing has become very beneficial for me, and I can't seem to type fast enough sometimes. The words just flow out of my mind.

On days when I find myself with too much time on my hands, I write. Other days I don't have a spare minute, and yet still have the time to write down an idea or two for later. I seem to be always thinking about or writing my next piece.

The main thing The Compassionate Friends taught me is to go on living my life and enjoying the child I have left, as well as my husband. And I have. I don't know what I would have done with my life if it weren't for those two very special people—my beautiful little daughter and my handsome husband, for whom my heart abounds with love. My daughter has kept me "together" since Benjie's death. We have managed to keep his memory alive for her sake, as well as our own, which has been very rewarding for me. There are still times that I find myself in disbelief that he's gone. Sometimes it's hard to believe that he ever existed. He was here for such a short time, and yet did so much in that brief time. He left an impression on so many people. I still feel a little guilty for not letting him do some of the things that he wanted to do. I look back now and ask myself, "Why didn't I let him do it?" I always thought we could do it tomorrow, but hindsight, as they say, is 20-20. For Benjie and us, there are no more tomorrows, only yesterdays. I find myself indulging my daughter. Am I being selfish? I don't know. All I know is that I now live my life a day at a time, sometimes an hour at a time. When my husband comes home from the road, our time together is precious. We spend it in ways that other families might find bizarre or weird. But when you're a truck driving/bereaved family, you have to make the most of every second because you never again want to take anyone or anything for granted. MAKE EVERY SECOND COUNT!!!

As a bereaved parent, I am often criticized for smiling or laughing about something. Although Benjie is dead, I am still allowed to be happy. Bereaved parents are entitled to the same happiness they had before their child's death. Being bereaved doesn't mean being sad all the time. We are human, and we still have the range of emotions that every other parent has.

Losing Benjie the way we did makes me appreciate the things and the loved ones I have even more. I don't take tomorrow for granted, but live for today.

Chapter 16

Fourth Birthday

Naturally, Benjie's fourth birthday was not a fun day. So how did we observe our son's fourth birthday? Benjamin Lee Taylor's fourth birthday was observed at the Santa Ana Cemetery with the placement of the headstone on his grave. We put flowers down and some balloons. We have a picture of our son on his fourth birthday. It's a photo of his headstone. That was a rude awakening and almost as hard to take as his death. Every time I go to his grave, it drives home a hard reality check.

I'm sure that any bereaved parent can say the same thing. You often feel that the dead child is just not home right now. But that "right now" feeling only lingers until you go to the cemetery, and the death hits you again like a ton of bricks.

There were no cheers, only flowers and tears that day. We will never again sing Happy Birthday to our son; at least not so he can hear it.

We will always just take flowers and balloons to our son. His favorite colors were blue and red, so I try to get balloons and flowers in those colors. His favorite flower was the carnation for two reasons: it is my birth month flower, and he didn't like roses because of the stickers, or thorns. He liked the color red because it is his father's and my favorite color.

It wouldn't be until October 26, 1997, that we would celebrate the fourth birthday of our living child, our daughter Tiffany. When she awoke that morning in a hotel room in San Diego, I said, in tears, to Buster, "Don't look now Daddy, but we have a four-year-old."

We have a family "joke" that it took me seven years to become the mother of a four year old.

Chapter 17

Tiffany's First Birthday

Tiffany's first birthday was almost as difficult as Benjie's fourth. However, Buster wasn't able to come home for Tiffany's birthday. He was on the road, earning a living for his family, as he still does today.

Benjie's absence was felt by everyone. The house, full of children, seemed empty to us. The little boy who had literally watched his sister being born was not there to help her celebrate her first birthday. He would have been so proud of her, and as protective as he had been for the first ten months of her life.

We got through the party and the day. We lit a candle in Benjie's memory and ended the day with a visit to his grave.

Chapter 18

First Holidays

The first holidays since Benjie's death were the hardest of all to face. For the first time in my life, I found myself in a cemetery on both Thanksgiving and Christmas Day in 1994. Buster was home for both holidays, because they were the first ones without Benjie.

As with many bereaved parents, traditions were not followed. We didn't have the traditional turkey and dressing for either holiday; instead we had prime rib and horseradish sauce.

No one was eager to open their gifts that Christmas, but we tried to keep things normal for Tiffany's sake. It's times like these that make having other children, especially young ones, hard to bear. But she has as much right to enjoy the holidays as we have to wish they wouldn't come.

We got through the holidays and began the new year.

Chapter 19

A Promise Kept

On August 23, 1994, I contacted an attorney with whom I used to work. I asked him about the possibilities of filing a wrongful death lawsuit against the apartment complex in Las Vegas. He told me I had the grounds but didn't feel he could handle it the way he felt we deserved. He, instead, gave me some names and numbers of other attorneys he felt would better serve our needs.

We got in touch with an attorney who turned out to be very well respected and known by my brother. He told us that since it occurred in Las Vegas, he couldn't help us but an associate of his in Las Vegas could.

On August 24, 1994, we contacted Attorney Cal J. Potter III and made an appointment to meet with him in his office on August 31, 1994 at 10 a.m. I remember telling him, "Just tell me when and where and we'll be there."

There we were at 10 a.m. sitting in the waiting room of Potter Law offices and then talking to Mr. Cal J. Potter himself.

We were both touched that he himself took our case instead of delegating it to one of his associates.

In June, 1995, a lawsuit was filed in the District Court, Clark County, Nevada. From then on, things started to pick up a bit.

I left Tiffany with a friend while I flew over to Las Vegas on April 24, 1996, and flew home early the next evening. Buster flew in from off the road. We met at the airport and went together to our hotel. We stayed at the Palace Station Hotel/Casino. We had a beautiful room. Buster flew out after I did the next night and went back on the road again.

On April 25, 1996, Buster and I were deposed by the attorney representing the owner and management company of our apartment complex. Before we went to his office, Mr. Potter informed us about what we were going to do. We saw a short video on the dos and don'ts of deposition taking. I went first and it was a 2 $^1/_2$ hour session. Buster was deposed after lunch for 1 $^1/_2$ hours.

During my deposition, the attorney asked me a question that put me in tears. Buster told me later that I had the whole room in tears (Mr. Potter, their attorney, the court reporter, and him) with my response. I must say I got some satisfaction with that news.

Again in April, two years later, Buster and I were deposed. It was on the 17th. The attorneys, this time around, represented the manufacturer and retailer of the vertical blinds that killed our son. The owner's and management's attorney was also in attendance. This time Buster insisted that we take Tiffany with us and so we did. We rented a car, a white Cadillac, and drove over. We stayed at the Boulder Station Hotel/Casino.

Buster was deposed first and it was a full morning's session. I took Tiffany out and kept her entertained. Buster's deposition took longer than anyone anticipated, going into the afternoon. Afterward, we went to lunch with our attorney so that he could clue me in to the questions that they might ask me based on Buster's testimony.

When it came time for my deposition, Tiffany cried because she had to go with her daddy and leave me behind. She had a ball with her daddy, seeing the dolphins and the white tigers at the Mirage Hotel on the Strip. I heard all about it when they returned.

After my deposition was over, before I even got up from the table, the retailer's attorney asked if he could speak to Mr. Potter. I went out to the waiting room and put my head down on the counter. Mr. Potter emerged from the room with a big smile on his face. He told Buster he could see the end in sight. He also asked if I was all right and Buster told him I was. I asked if I did okay, and he told me I did just fine. We drove home the next day.

In April of 1999, Linda, a paralegal in the Potter offices, informed me that a trial date had been set for July 12, 1999. However, it would not be a good idea to bring Tiffany along this time. I happened to mention this to a teacher at Tiffany's school who in turn told Tiffany's teacher, and, before I knew it, Tiffany had a place to stay for a week with her teacher, Joyce Unwin, and her family. I have to say Joyce Unwin is an exceptional teacher and extraordinary friend. Tiffany adores her and so do I. All I had to do was say I needed help and she gave it.

On April 12, 1999, we accepted a partial settlement offer from the retailer as the evidence proving their liability had been inconclusive. Our complex's owner apparently bought from many retailers so a good faith offer was made and we accepted it.

David Arsenault, one of Cal Potter's associates, called me on Monday, May 10th, just before 1:45 p.m. He left a message and I returned his call as soon as I got the message since he had said it was very important. I did that no later than 1:50 p.m. A mediation meeting had been arranged for Saturday, June 5th. He wanted to know if we would be available that day and I told him that we wouldn't because that was the day of Tiffany's dance recital. I told him the 12th would be fine or any Saturday after that. He told me he would get back to me about the 12th.

On Tuesday, May 11th, I called David back regarding the 12th of June. I was told it was no good. I said the 19th or 26th would be fine. He'd let me know by the end of the week.

On Thursday, May 13th, I called David again since Buster was home for Tiffany's school's Open House and we wanted a firm date. David then asked if Linda had called and I told him she hadn't. (I found out later she left a message on the machine.) David told me that the 19th and 26th of June were out. It would have to be this month. I told him Mondays are bad but that would be fine.

David called us back that day around 2 p.m. to say that the meeting would have to be on June 5th if at all possible. After crying about it, I agreed and we made the arrangements. Later I had to tell Tiffany that Mommy and Daddy would not be able to be at her dance recital. A school friend and his mother would take her to dress rehearsal and then her teacher, Joyce Unwin, would take her for the weekend as well as to the recital. Tiffany took it all in stride and was not at all upset about it. I was more upset than she was. Her response to me was a very mature one. She simply stated, "That's okay Mommy. It's for Benjie."

Tiffany's whole life had been embroiled in this lawsuit and she was just taking it on the chin one more time. She would be rewarded for her generosity.

On the 21st of May, I called David with some questions about the latest invoice and he told me that the entire office was very optimistic about the outcome of June 5th. That made me feel a lot better.

A week later, I called David again with some more questions. He called me back to inform me that the 5th of June was out and the 26th of June was in. Hadn't I been informed of that with a letter he wrote? I told him I hadn't the slightest idea of the change. I was told that the other side could not get authorization to make a settlement until the 26th. I told David we already had the reservations and were set to come to Las Vegas on the 4th of June. He told me he would get it all nailed down and get back to me on Tuesday, the 1st of June, since Monday was Memorial Day.

I ended up calling on the 1st and asked Linda to call me back. She did within the hour. The 26th was in because the other side's insurance company would not be able to get the money together until the 26th. Linda then informed me that a letter to that effect would be mailed to my attention that day. David later called to tell me the same thing. When Buster called, I told him. I then changed all our reservations and I had that done before noon.

Linda called me the morning of the 7th of June to ask if I had received the overnight letter from their office. I said no, what letter? To get the partial settlement, we had to sign a release and get it back to them by overnight delivery. I got hold of an upset Buster who just happened to be in Las Vegas on his way to Ontario, California, with a load. After several phone calls from him, to him, from Mr. Potter's office, to his office, and finally, to the overnight delivery service, we found that the letter had been delivered around 3:30 p.m. with no knock on the door or ringing of the doorbell. In the meantime, Buster had gotten home around noon and sat and waited. By 4:30 p.m. we were having our signatures notarized and had the form back in the drop box to Mr. Potter's office and us home again by 5 p.m. Buster left shortly thereafter.

On the 8th of June, I called and talked with Jewelene in Mr. Potter's office and asked her about getting some of the money from the partial settlement. She told me that Mr. Potter had been planning to send us some of it anyway. I told her that the release was on its way back to them as of 5 p.m. on the 7th and she thanked me. We chatted for a few minutes. I told her about Linda's suggestion to bring photos of Benjie and she thought it was a very good one. Let the people see what a beautiful little boy he was. I mentioned the last photo and she asked when it was taken. I told her two days before or five hours before the accident from which he would not recover. She said to make sure they knew that when they saw the picture. I said, "Good, I'll do just that." We concluded our phone call after about 15 minutes. It was great to be able to talk with Jewelene again. After all, she had been the first one we met in Mr. Potter's office that first day.

On the 9th, Linda called me after hours and left a message on my machine as I was not home at the time. I called back just before 6 p.m. to find her gone for the day. Instead, I talked with Jewelene once again. She told me that we had to have a Power of Attorney signed and notarized before they could deposit the check into a trust fund so we could get our share of it. They would send it to me overnight and I would return it to them the same way.

The next day I called and talked with Linda. She was preparing separate Power of Attorney forms for Buster and me. I received them on the 11th, which was also our 11th wedding anniversary. I signed mine and had it back in the drop box that afternoon. In the meantime, I called and asked David if they had a separate form for Buster to sign should he get through Las Vegas before we arrived for the mediation meeting on the 26th. He said they did.

Linda called me on the morning of the 23rd to say they had nothing in the files about funeral and burial costs for Benjamin. She asked if I could get some copies and send them. I told her I would call Saddleback Chapel and have them get on it. She gave me the office fax number so they could fax it to them. In the meantime, I called Santa Ana Cemetery to ask for the same and they called me back with the information which I later picked up. A few hours after my initial phone call, Saddleback Chapel called saying they had the requested information and I asked if they would fax it for me. They agreed. I then called Linda with the news and she told David to expect it. I would bring any further information with me.

Tiffany was fine when we left for Las Vegas in a rental car, a pewter-colored Lincoln Town Car, around 10 a.m. on the 25th of June. We left her with a neighbor. This was the same neighbor and friend who not only had helped us get the apartment in Las Vegas but with whom I had grown up.

We reached Barstow, California, by 11:40 a.m. It was already 94° and very windy. Buster had lunch. My nerves wouldn't let me eat or drink anything the entire drive that day.

By 1 p.m., we were in the 103° heat in Baker, California. On the highway, the temperature was already a blistering 108°. By 1:45 p.m., we were at the Nevada state line. After that, I just sat back and tried to relax, thinking all the while about my Benjie, wondering what he'd look like now, what all his favorites would be.

We arrived at our hotel, Circus Circus, and checked in. We had a 3 p.m. appointment at Mr. Potter's office so we didn't even go to out room until afterward. We got there on time and went into the conference room where the meeting would take place the next morning. By the end of that hour, I was in tears. We learned that one of the opposing attorneys was after me like a dog guarding a bone.

The next morning we left our hotel room and it was already 85° at 7:30 a.m. We drove around town until 8 a.m. when we had to be at Mr. Potter's office where, upon our arrival, we received our partial settlement check. I talked to Linda for a few minutes and asked her for a hug, which she gladly gave me. She then told me that if I needed to take a break at any time during the coming hours, to come looking for her on the other side of the building.

Everyone arrived by 8:30 a.m. or a little later. The mediator, Mr. Jim Armstrong, opened the meeting with all of us sitting around the table in the conference room. He explained the procedures of mediation and how he felt about the case. He told us a little bit about himself, as well. He had been on vacation and gotten home a week before, using that week to bring himself up to par on the facts of the case. He went on to tell us that he had been practicing law for 22 years and mediating cases for 7 years. He had a 90% success rate of settling cases that he mediated. He felt ours would be one of them.

By 9 a.m., Buster and I were in Mr. Potter's private office with him and Mr. Armstrong where we remained for the duration. Mr. Armstrong would go back and forth between the two parties trying to resolve the matter.

I did take Linda up on her offer and visited her in her office. It was good to get away from the stress and the strain of the session. We talked about what I was going through emotionally, the case itself, and our families. When I thought I had stayed away long enough, I rejoined Buster and Mr. Potter.

At 3 p.m. after 6 hours and no lunch, a settlement amount was reached. A brief hand-written agreement was then drawn up by Mr. Armstrong stating the amount and date this case would be paid—July 15, 1999. Then the paper was passed around the room for Buster, Mr. Potter, and me to sign. It was then taken to the conference room where the opposing attorneys and their agents also signed it. We then received a copy of the completed document.

As I signed this form and later got a copy, I told Mr. Armstrong that he reminded me of the actor, Frank Aletter, who he did not know. Mr. Armstrong was a very distinguished looking gentleman with a beard. I liked him. He showed us great compassion.

We left Mr. Potter's office without seeing the other attorneys again. Mr. Potter kept us in seclusion since he didn't want to see them either. He asked Linda to tell him when they were gone. We left his office after 3:30 p.m., but not before thanking everyone there for all the work and time they had put into our case.

All the way back to the hotel room, I kept saying, amidst my tears: "I kept my promise. I kept my promise."

We had promised to bring something home for Tiffany. When asked what she wanted, she said a teddy bear, a purple teddy bear. After dinner at the Excalibur Buffet, we purchased a teddy bear in one of the gift shops. It was dressed in a purple damsel dress with a pointed-tasseled hat.

By 8 p.m. that evening, I was so relaxed I was ready to fall asleep. I slept very well that night for the first time in years.

We were up early the next morning, the 27th of June, and left Las Vegas by 7:30 a.m. We stopped at the Nevada Landing Hotel/Casino where Buster had something to eat. I looked around while he ate. We left there around 8:30 a.m. We reached the California state line shortly after 9 a.m.

Around 11:15 a.m., we got into bumper-to-bumper traffic in Ontario, California, due to roadwork. The temperature was only 76° in the area. A turnoff from the freeway on which we were traveling was closed and we had a detour to a side street a couple of miles down the road. That lasted about 15 minutes for us. By 11:37 a.m., we were on the next leg of our journey home. Ten minutes later, we were stopped again due to an accident being cleared from the carpool lane. Once we were past that, we sailed on.

As we got closer to our freeway turnoff for home, I was thinking how nice it would be if we could stop by the grave. Apparently Buster was thinking the same thing, because he took the turnoff prior to ours and headed in that direction. I told him that we were both thinking the same thing and thanked him. A few minutes later we pulled into the cemetery and drove to our son's grave.

As we got out of the car, I was a bit stiff from sitting for 3 1/2 hours. Buster had gone ahead to have a few moments alone with our son. I often give him that since he doesn't have the daily opportunities to visit that I do. As I got to the grave, I stopped, started crying, and knelt down to talk to Benjie. I said, "It took me almost five years, Baby, but Mama did it. I kept my promise." We stayed a few minutes longer and then went home to see Tiffany. We were home by 12:30 p.m. on Sunday, June 27, 1999.

When I got into the house, I called our neighbor to surprise Tiffany. When her daughter answered the phone, I said, "Hi, we're home and I really need to see and hold my girl."

She said to Tiffany, "Tiffy, your mom's home already."

I said goodbye, hung up, and hurried across the street. When the door opened, I grabbed Tiffany as soon as I saw her. I picked her up off her feet and just held her without saying a word. It seemed like forever to her but I couldn't hold Benjie anymore. When I told her that, she quit the little complaining she was doing and, instead, packed up all her things and raced home.

We spent about an hour together before we said our good-byes to Buster. He was back on the road again by 1:30 p.m. that afternoon.

On the 7th of July, I called and talked to Linda about the status of the releases and checks from the defendants' attorneys. In the meantime, we would not have to sign anything more because of the Power of Attorney forms we signed earlier. We would, however, have to sign off on all the bills created by this case.

On the 15th, I signed off on the bills and had the form back to Linda via overnight delivery.

Buster went into the Potter offices on the 19th of July and signed the same form. I received the settlement check on the 20th of July and deposited it into the bank.

Our case was finally won. All along, we had the questions of why we did it. Based on those questions, I wrote a statement that I had hoped could be read after the mediation meeting was over, but that didn't happen. It read as follows:

> We did not bring this lawsuit for the money. All the money in the world won't bring our son back to us where he belongs. I would gladly give up all my possessions to have BOTH my children in my life for my children are my life and my future. Half of my future is gone.
>
> Instead, we did this so that other parents don't have to go through what we've had to endure. We must make the American businessman, i.e., manufacturers, retailers, and landlords, more responsible for their products. We must make them more aware of the American family's right to safety, especially that of our children. For another child to die in this manner would be barbaric.

When we rented that apartment in Las Vegas on the 15th of December, 1993, we believed that we would live there for years. We believed that the landlord would make sure that our new home would be safe for our children. If it had been, Benjie would not be where is now, but instead with me, alive and well.

To give us a sense of closure, I arranged a part of celebration to be held on the eve of Benjamin Lee Taylor's 5th anniversary. The date of this party was August 21, 1999. I know Benjie would be happy. I invited all the friends I could think of. Some were from school, some from TCF, and some from before he died. Tiffany's teacher, Joyce Unwin, came as well as the first person I met at my first PTO meeting, Alison Horner, and her family. Tiffany is in her daughter's scout troop and they are good friends, as well. My friend, Paula, was our hostess for the evening. One family from TCF was there, too. They arrived a little after dark.

During the course of the party, I made a toast to Benjie. There were tears following this toast but they weren't just in my eyes. It went like this:

> Needless to say, Buster and I are relieved to have all this behind us. We want to thank Paula Theida for this wonderful party, her father, Tom Becker, for allowing us the use of his home and to all our friends and family who helped maintain us through this ordeal. It's been a rough and long road but we knew of its length from the beginning. Some friends couldn't be here tonight but are here in spirit.
>
> Now, I'd like you to raise your drinks in a toast. To our beloved Benjie: you were the best little boy who ever lived. We love and miss you. I kept my promise Baby. TO BENJIE!!

One thing I do know. I was finally able to keep the last promise I ever made to my son. I made that promise to him as I sat at his graveside during that part of his funeral. I promised that someday someone would pay for what they did to him.

There's one thing I've always done with my children. I never break a promise to them. When I make a promise, I KEEP it!!

Chapter 20

My Thoughts

The following pages contain various "quotes," poems, and articles I have written in my journey through my grief. They were written to ease my pain, to help others, and to express how I was feeling. Some are based on an occasion or a holiday. All are based on my grief. I hope they will help others to understand how it feels to lose a child.

A MESSAGE TO THE NONBEREAVED
Attention People:

I am a bereaved parent. My almost four year-old son died accidentally. Many of my friends are also bereaved parents. Please don't punish us more by ignoring us or not letting us talk about our children. They existed, just as much as your children exist. They had dreams. We shared those dreams. They say that it's easier to deal with a problem when you talk about it. Why won't you let us talk about them? When we laugh, don't spurn us. Bereaved parents are allowed to laugh as much as we cry. Sometimes it's the only way we can keep our sanity. Don't begrudge us that small pleasure. For some, laughing is a way of hiding the pain.

Some of us feel that we have to go on for the sake of our surviving children. I know that I did. My daughter was only ten months old when her brother died. If it hadn't been for her, I would have preferred to lie down next to his grave and die too. However, I have come to the conclusion that I deserve to see at least one of my children grow up. She, in turn, deserves the same mother she had before her brother died. However, I'm not the same, and I never will be again.

I know a lot of people feel it can happen to them. Maybe that is true, but losing a child is not a disease. It is not contagious. You can not "catch" it from a bereaved parent. Circumstances in our daily lives produce the possibility, not people.

We look upon life differently now. As spring and the celebrations that come with it approach, I find myself with renewed strength, knowing that I will see my son again someday.

I laugh, and, yes, I still cry, because, you see, he lived. He laughed, he cried, but worst of all, he died.

* * *

B U D D Y

He was not my father, my brother, or my son,
But of us, he was one.
For almost two years, he was Benjie's best friend
Who stayed with him right to the end.
It's been three years and a lot of tears have been shed.
We couldn't bear to separate them so we put him with our son
In his eternal bed.
They were as inseparable as two can be.
You may ask—"What was his name? Who was he?"
The answer to that is easy.
To many, he was known as "Leonardo."
But to our son, he was simply "Buddy."

* * *

The difference between a parent and a bereaved parent is that the bereaved parent has to imagine life WITH his child. A parent doesn't.

* * *

A-U-G-U-S-T

August 22nd, our nightmare was born
Upon this hot Las Vegas morn.
God chose to take you away, our little son
Until we can be together again.
Seems like only yesterday but instead
Three years have come and gone since then.

* * *

MY SON

My son was a wonderful little boy
Who took great pride and care in each little toy.
He was thrilled in becoming a big brother
Who treated his little sister like there was no other.
One of his dreams was to go to school;
Instead she has learned to swim in a pool.
I looked forward to watching him grow to be a man,
Now all I have are memories to deal with as best I can.

* * *

A TRIBUTE TO MY FORGOTTEN CHILD

After the loss of a child, a parent tends to "tune out" the other children while grieving. I know that I did. My daughter was only ten months old when her brother died.

However, that soon changed. Tiffany became my focal point. Everything I do now is centered on her. She's in school now and dancing in a recital. She swims like a fish and will play soccer in the fall.

I do everything with her, so we've become more like girlfriends, in some cases, than mother and daughter. We tend to dress alike and watch TV together. I do for her what my mother did for me. I'm a room mom at school and a team mom on the field. She's my whole world and I'm hers.

She has her friends and I have mine, but when we're together, we're together. Our song is "You and Me Against the World" because that's how we feel sometimes. We're there for each other in any way we possibly can. You would be surprised how supportive a four year old can be when she wants to be.

So Sweetheart, I'm sorry you ever felt left out. You, like your brother, will never be my forgotten child.

* * *

Death is like a commencement ceremony, leaving one life for another, much like a high school graduate going on to college or a college graduate going out into the world of the working class.

As a commencement speaker, one might say that death is a part of our future, where we will once again meet the ones we've lost in our pasts and where our pasts will become the presence of not only gifts but of life.

BECAUSE OF YOU

Because of you,
we became a family.
Because of you,
our love had no boundary.
Because of you,
I have an ache that never ends.
Because of you,
I have made new friends.
Because of you,
I have learned to live and laugh again.
Because of you.

* * *

HE WAS ONLY A CHILD

He was only a child
conceived in love.
He was only a child,
a gift from above.
He was only a child
who wanted to grow old.
He was only a child
with a heart of gold.
He was only a child,
the apple of my eye.
He was only a child,
so why, oh why, did he have to die?
He was only a child.

* * *

Through my journey down the road called "GRIEF," I have found it to be like a cancer. I can find myself in a remission of sorts when I have a good time and forget my pain for a while. But then something happens, and that pain comes shooting vengefully back, a little milder than it was before.

* * *

YOUR LAST HALLOWEEN

You had just turned three,
You wanted to be a ninja turtle going door to door.
You'd beg and plea
So I took you to the store.

Living in an apartment complex as we did,
Daddy and I figured you'd get your fill and come home.
But once you caught on to the fun of it,
The more you wanted to roam.

I stayed home with your newborn sister,
We thought it best.
While Daddy went out with you, our little mister,
I was put to the test.

Now it's 1997, your fourth in heaven.
Little did we know that 1993
Would be your last Halloween.

* * *

THAT ROAD CALLED GRIEF

No matter where we may live,
nor where we may roam,
we all have a place we call home.
For some of us it be an arduous task
just getting through each day.
While others manage to keep our emotions
from getting in the way.
Unlike the yellow brick road,
which is long and winding,
the road called GRIEF can become a heavy load.
There's no time for a warning or any planning.
We just find ourselves making a very unhappy landing.
One minute we're happy, the next we could be sad.
For, if you let it, it can drive you mad, mad, MAD!
Although it may not have an end,
if you reach out, as I have, you may find yourself with more
than one Compassionate Friend.

* * *

THAT FIRST MEETING

You've just suffered the worst trauma of your life. Your child has died. The cause or the age of the child doesn't matter. He's dead. That's it.

Next you find yourself in a turmoil of emotions. What's next? What do you do? What should you do? What can you do? You'll find yourself surrounded by well-meaning friends and family who have their ideas about what you should do and how long it should take you to get through it. But unless they've been where you are right now, they haven't got a clue about how or what you're feeling. You may just want to sit and cry. You may just feel nothing but numb initially. You're in shock. How do you take it all in? How can you?

Maybe you'll make some calls, or somebody with real insight about your pain will give you a phone number for a support group called Compassionate Friends. You take the number and put it aside. Maybe you'll call later. Besides, how can anyone else know how you feel? After a while you do call, and you find out that it's a support group of other bereaved parents. You find out that you may not be so alone after all.

The next question you find yourself asking where and when are the meetings? To your amazement, you're asked where you live. There are chapters of the group all over your area. You find the one nearest you and decide to try it out. At least see what they have to offer. You have nothing more to lose. You've already lost your whole world, right?

The evening of the first meeting arrives. You walk in a little early. You didn't want to be late. You feel awkward enough just being there. You walk into a room where people are talking, laughing, even telling jokes. You feel compelled to ask, "Is this the Compassionate Friends?" The answer is, surprisingly, yes, and you are immediately given a warm welcome by a person who is identified as the chapter leader. You may ask if the person with whom you spoke on the phone is there, and then want to sit near that person. That's fine with everyone. They want you to feel at ease. You're told what occurs at these meetings, what they're all about, their purpose, and what is expected of you. What is expected of you is nothing—nothing at all. You've made the first step already. You came to your first meeting. That took a lot of courage, and you're commended for it. They'll tell you that introductions are made. The chapter leader will identify him or herself, tell the group about his or her child, how he or she died, maybe how long ago, maybe what the circumstances surrounding the death were. If you want to speak, you do. If you don't, you don't. You soon find that this is one place where you can do or say anything and not be judged or ridiculed. If you want to get angry, SHOW it. If you want to cry, DO it. You'll feel better for it, and you'll have many understanding friends in the room to support you.

Before you know it, the meeting is over, and you may find yourself asking when the next one will be. You look forward to it, knowing how good the first one made you feel.

The months go by, and you've now attended three or more meetings. You see new people coming to the meetings, asking the same questions that you did. Only this time, you may be the one to offer some of the answers to their questions. You've learned as we all have, that it's okay to smile, chuckle, or even laugh. And, yes, you will laugh again. There's no timetable as to when or how soon, but there will come a day when you'll be looking in the mirror, and instead of tears on your face, you will see a smile. You may have to do a double-take, but it will be there. Just as our children had to sit before they could stand, walk before they could run in their journey through life, so do we in our journey through grief.

And, to think, it all started at that first meeting.

* * *

AN "INDEPENDENT" THOUGHT

Isn't that the day we declared ourselves independent of
England? Why can't we do that with our grief? Do we really
want to? Would we if we could? If we did, would we also be
declaring our independence from our memories of our
child? Would we want to if we could? Wouldn't it be wonderful to be able to rid ourselves of the grief and its control
of us and keep the loving memories locked away in a safe
and secure part of our hearts? Be we can't, and we won't,
because to do that we must deny ourselves the love and
devotion that we gave and received from that child while he
or she was with us. But, then, isn't that what love is all
about? This is one independence that just can't be declared.
Grief just comes with the territory.

* * *